# THE DOWBEATERS

**Other books by Ira U. Cobleigh, A.B., A.M., ScD.**

# THE DOWBEATERS

## How to Buy Stocks That Go Up

### by Ira U. Cobleigh and Bruce K. Dorfman

**Macmillan Publishing Co., Inc**

New York

**Collier Macmillan Publishers**

London

Macmillan Publishing Co., Inc.
866 Third Avenue
New York, N.Y. 10022
Collier Macmillan Canada, Ltd.

Library of Congress Cataloging in Publication Data
Cobleigh, Ira U.
The Dowbeaters.
Bibliography: p.
1. Stocks—United States.    2. Investments—United States.    I. Dorfman, Bruce K., joint author.    II. Title.
HG4921.C595    1979    332.6′322    79-997
ISBN 0-02-526500-8

9   8   7   6   5   4   3

Designed by Jack Meserole

Printed in the United States of America

Dedicated to
Truth, Justice, and the
American Way . . .

# Contents

## PART THREE
## DOWBEATER INVESTMENTS

## PART FOUR
## DOWBEATER SPECULATIONS

# Acknowledgments

Half of this book and many complete chapters reflect the patient research and actual writing of my friend and colleague Bruce K. Dorfman. Bruce's insights on market motions and prophetic vision of major trends are indispensable to the message of *The Dowbeaters*.

IRA U. COBLEIGH

The concepts explored in this book were advanced with the research and assistance of the following individuals and corporations:

Agnico Eagle Mines Ltd.              Paul Penna, president
Arnold Bernhard & Co., Value         Arnold Bernhard, president
    Line Investment Survey

Acknowledgments  x

| | |
|---|---|
| Bear, Stearns & Co. | Kingsley C. Barham |
| Bishop, Rosen & Co. | Thomas J. Herzfeld, executive vice-president |
| Callas, Powell, Rosenthal & Bloch | Daniel Rosenthal, vice-president |
| Dean Witter Reynolds Inc. | Charles Moskowitz, Ted Kepreos |
| Discom Securities, Inc. | Brian Terasuk, Stuart Wolfe |
| Dow Theory Letters, Inc. | Richard Russell, president |
| Dowbeaters, Inc. | Peter DeAngelis |
| First Boston | Paul D. Sonz |
| First Jersey Securities Co. | Robert Berkson, vice-president |
| The Hirsch Organization | Yale Hirsch, president |
| E. F. Hutton & Co. | Arthur Barzilay |
| Investment Quality Trends | K. Weiss, G. Weiss |
| Investor's Research | K. Hagen |
| International Trading Group Ltd. | David C. Beare, chairman of the board |
| Lowe Investment Financial Letter | Chris Lowe, president |
| Lowry's Reports | Paul Desmond, president |
| Lynch International Investment Survey | Walter A. Lynch |
| Macmillan Publishing Co., Inc. | Joyce Jack, editor |
| *The Market Chronicle* | Claude D. Seibert, publisher |
| Merrill Lynch, Pierce, Fenner & Smith, Inc. | Wallace Sellers, vice-president |
| Rockwell, DeWitt, Conklin Organization | Henry Rockwell, president |
| *The Silver and Gold Report* | James R. Blakeley |
| Trendline Division of Standard & Poor's | Ken Lutz, president |
| *Wall Street Week* | Frank Capiello |

BRUCE K. DORFMAN

# PART ONE
# DOWBEATER
# TIMING

# ☐

# America at

# Book Value!

*Are you prepared for the coming explosive stock-market boom?*

The Dowbeaters represents a milestone in investment conceptualization. It marks the end of one of Wall Street's most massive bear markets and heralds one of the greatest investment opportunities in over a generation.

*Do you have an investment plan?*

This book is as pragmatic as it is profound. *The Dowbeaters*, utilizing the world-renowned Dow Jones Industrial Average to measure the pulse of the American economy, takes an evolutionary leap from present-day investment philosophies. No one method, technique, stock, or stock group is absolute. *The Dowbeaters* builds multilevel investment strategies for those who can seize the opportunity of a unique investment juncture for America. This is a time that affords investors maximum opportunity with minimal risks—a time that finds the subtle positive winds of economic change unnoticed by panic-stricken investors.

This exciting Wall Street adventure into economic time will show you how to invest when most are apathetic and pessimistic, extrapolating our present economic plight into oblivion. The book utilizes the strengths of tested investment-management techniques and timing methods for those investors seeking to compound their investment capital in the coming decade.

*The Dowbeaters* is multidimensional; it represents the great fundamental and technical research available today. It is the synthesis of decades of research in actual application by Wall Street professionals. It is a book that is purposely being released at a unique time for investors.

*Are you interested in fast speculative gain?*

*The Dowbeaters* presents a broad spectrum of investment techniques. Not only will this book show you how to compound and build investment capital throughout bull and bear markets, but it also identifies the scores of stocks we feel are most likely to outperform the Dow averages during the market's forthcoming price explosion. And for speculators with the patience and courage to participate in low-priced stock speculation, we select specific mini-stocks.

*Do you know how the economic forces of supply and demand are operating to create the coming price explosion in the Dow averages?*

*The Dowbeaters* identifies the catalysts for the coming bull market which will explode prices to new all-time highs. The catalysts are masked in today's negative investment environment, but are about to launch the Dow Averages into headline news, day after day, as record millions join the rush to own common stocks.

*Are you concerned about the potential risks in investing?*

*The Dowbeaters* has a specific plan that is virtually risk-free. You will find out how the rich get richer. This plan is ideal for the coming decade and can give you the peace of mind necessary to any successful investment program.

*Do you want to eliminate emotion from investing?*

This book goes right to the core of investing psychology. We show the fundamental investment parameters that have existed throughout this century. *The Dowbeaters* shows the continual value relationships that motivate stock prices, and how to identify strategic times to invest for low-risk, high-gain returns.

*The Dowbeaters* is more than an investment guide. It is a book that can cornerstone your entire financial future. It will show you the counterbalancing forces that are acting to undermine the economic negatives of today's inflation and economic stagnation. You will have a roadmap for the future to help you anticipate, instead of react. This book will help you score significant gains on Wall Street and improve your net worth. This book will show you how to buy stocks that go up!

## America at Book Value!

America, as revealed through the message of the Dow Jones Industrial Average, is for sale at book value or below today! At only a few times in Dow history has America sold below book value. Each time has flashed a remarkable investment opportunity—a golden opportunity for investors to have their cake and eat it too! This is an opportunity to buy and hold; to receive both dividends and long-term capital gains; to build fortunes in low-priced stocks. When an investor buys at book value, he is buying today's assets and not tomorrow's promises. He is not speculating on the unknown. He is buying, in many cases, liquid tangible corporate assets for sixty-five and seventy-five cents on the dollar.

Here are the few select times when the Dow has sold below book value in the past fifty years:

| | | |
|---|---|---|
| July 1932 | Dow 41.22 | The low point of the Depression and the low year of the century for the Dow Averages. |
| April 1942 | Dow 92.92 | World War II had undermined the future security of the United States. |
| June 1949 | Dow 160.62 | Postwar recessionary fears were being extrapolated into a Depression. |
| December 1974 | Dow 577.60 | Watergate had created a credibility crisis for the dollar. Depression thought imminent. |

October 1978     Dow 789.67     Monetary crisis heats up, creating fear of all paper mediums. The dollar at all-time lows against many major currencies.

Now, amidst inflation, recession, and languid public pessimism, stocks are being moved into the hands of the "few." These financial elite are gobbling up the stock certificates of American corporations and locking them away in their bank vaults. This is happening now while the light of reason is concealed from most investors by dark, overhanging economic clouds. These clouds obscure the true economic picture and the potentials for an economic turnaround on a grand scale.

As day follows night, the crowd's negative economic mood is certain to end, as does every economic phase. By reflection and insight, which you will gain from reading this book, you can separate yourself from current negative thinking.

Naturally, when there is little confidence in our economic system, stock prices remain low. Without bear markets or long sideways "wearing-out" periods how could stocks be priced favorably enough for the few to accumulate, in order that they may sell to the many later, when the inexorable cyclical swing powerfully inflates the levels of stock prices?

Panic waves of fear and uncertainty, occurring with cyclical regularity, have repeatedly driven the prices of stocks down to rewarding buying levels throughout history. Few realize that the major economic problems of today are difficult more because of our subjectivity than their reality.

For example, our main current economic problem, inflation, reached comparable intensity both in 1921 and 1949.

The problems that we solved in the post-World War II era were actually not very different from the ones that plague us today. Then, as now, postwar inflation was linked with a stale, stagnant economy. (From a historical perspective, inflations have frequently preceded booms and *not* led to the political and social unrest that is currently thought likely. What we are plagued with—what dominates our economy and the whole system of capitalism—is a major lack of faith in man for his fellow man and in the basic paper mediums used to conduct business.) Now, due to inflation fears, the dollar, stocks, and bonds are being dumped at historically low levels of valuation. Many market observers have become so gloomy that they predict a depression ahead, or even a complete breakdown of our economic system. But what investors don't realize is that right now, major positive forces are emerging as a result of the dramatic shifts in valuations of the dollar on the world currency market.

As these signs become readily apparent, the grand bull market will be unfolding. Since 1966, the Dow Jones has failed to make any major progress on the upside. It seems now, though, that the final stages of the bear market are about to end. In the next decade, we will find that the dollar will be low enough to ignite an explosive export boom. We will then begin a major bull market in the dollar.

The fact is that the dollar is in a supply/demand market like the stock market, where it rises and falls. At some point the dollar will sink to a low enough plateau to make American goods and services competitive once again. This will begin the grand economic upmove. The grand upmove will find major devaluations against the dollar, as it soars and all other currencies fall against it.

Because of the fall of the US dollar right now, our goods, services, and labor are becoming proportionately cheaper worldwide. Our current situation can be compared to the post-World War II boom in Japan and Germany, the result of their currencies going to very low levels on the world markets. This was the catalyst to their export booms.

With the fall of the dollar, we are observing a steady rise in the cost of foreign products. Cars, radios, cameras, and other products that have been exported to the USA in massive quantities have now finally reached price levels where they are less competitive with our domestic products, simply because of major shifts in currency valuation.

The result of the dramatic devaluation of our dollar will be a new grand-scale supercycle bull market. This move will launch many stocks into 1000 percent moves in the new climate. This climate will heat up again as the world begins its rush to buy America at book value.

*The Dowbeaters* is based on the belief that with a new economic ground swell, the methods and companies identified in this book will ride the crest of this wave into the new decade. Lightning is about to strike!

The book value, earnings, and dividends of the Dow Averages have doubled since 1964, but the Dow quotations have not advanced to mirror these higher values. For the last fifteen years, each and every year has found the Dow in the 800–900 zone at some time. Since this same period has contained such a massive fundamental growth leap in dividends and earnings, we feel that the Dow is now at bedrock levels. (See centerfold for a complete, long-term illustration of these value relationships.)

Along with this internal fundamental growth, we have also witnessed a soaring gross national product. This has occurred in spite of five presidents in fifteen years, a war, an inflation, and mass public pessimism. One set of negatives after another, yet the Dow is at the same levels and is fundamentally stronger than ever!

This is therefore a confident book designed to dispel gloom and to view in the distance the return of a vibrant capitalistic economy, affording once again fortune-building opportunities in the stock market such as existed in such profusion in the post-World War II boom.

We predict a renaissance of exuberance in the stock market—a renewed zeal for speculation in the 1980s. America will overcome its inertia, bounce back, and resume its earlier pre-eminence in productive efficiency and its traditional leadership in technological breakthroughs.

We predict a bull market of the grandest proportions, which will move the Dow Average to 2000 or higher! Here we explain how you can profit from this new investment climate, and outline the rules for accumulating an appropriate portfolio of stocks. The strategies given in this book will cover the investment spectrum from conservative to very speculative.

This book differs from most on securities and investment because it uses the Dow Jones Industrial Average alone as its constant point of reference. We suggest a continuing comparison between the market performance of individual stocks and/or a portfolio and the performance of the DJIA.

To be a "Dowbeater," a stock, researched to blend income with capital gain, must consistently outpace "the Dow." If in addition the stock should double or triple in price, is split, or increases its dividend—then so much the better!

It is our sincere belief that it is possible to identify superior action stocks through incisive research and using the following time-tested criteria. Such stocks should, in general:

1. be in uptick or "turnaround" industries;
2. evidence rising earning power;
3. have a positive technical chart;
4. sell below the prevailing DJIA multiple;
5. trade in active volume;
6. be low priced, preferably below $20, for animate market motion;
7. have some special attraction likely to stimulate market interest;
8. have an energetic, innovative, and stock-owning management;
9. in certain cases, be an acquisition candidate;
10. earn 12 percent or more on stockholders' equity;
11. document a growth rate of 12 percent or more annually; and
12. relate to a young company with unusual products and a small capitalization.

Investments with most of these characteristics have usually performed well in the past and appear likely to continue doing so in the future.

We stress the importance of low multiples because of the costly mistakes made by even sophisticated investors (individual as well as institutional) who in 1968–72 found themselves paying forty to sixty times earnings for glamour stocks—to their great sorrow.

Thus, in recent years, there have been myriads of investors whose results in Wall Street have proved disappointing. Whereas in 1968 there were approximately 30 million common stockholders in America, according to a recent NYSE calculation, by 1977 that number had shrunk to 25 million —a loss of 5 million! There are myriads more who would like to enter the market now (and, incidentally, expand the reservoir of equity capital in America) should they encounter a dependable method for screening securities.

There are basically four separate investment philosophies we recommend, any one of which, intelligently pursued, should prove rewarding over time: the Eclipse Method, the Herzfeld Hedge, the Dowbeater Stocks and Bonds, and the Dowbeater Speculations. You will find each method unique and capable of standing on its own strengths—you can select the one that appeals most to your investment philosophy. You will also find that you can combine methods to customize a strategy that will attain the long-term financial rewards possible in the 1980s.

By the early 1980s, the press, radio, and television will again exude bullishness. A mood of optimism will surface, as the DJIA travels zestfully to new all-time highs. The stock market again will be center stage as a topic of conversation; the speculative languor of the past few years will fade away. New stories of corporate gain and glamour will be bruited about; new stocks, tips, and rumors will animate and motivate market action.

Wall Street will hum, as the crowd reverses its viewpoint

and new investors awake to the coming era. Enter the brave bulls, with herds of sheep following them. For most investors, the roar of the crowd and the trading volume that accompanies high prices are just what is needed for them to join the rush. But the greatest success will come only to those few who can apply logic and patience to investment decisions and who act in the vanguard of the economy's next move. Wake up, America!

"Looks like the small investor is finally getting back into the market." (*Drawing by Chas. Addams;* © *1976 The New Yorker Magazine, Inc.*)

# 2

# The Grand American
# Economic Supercycle

History shows us that our nation's economy has operated on a grand supercycle throughout this century. This supercycle, which seems to span several decades, has four phases. The first phase is war: During wartimes, the nation's efforts are directed toward defense and armaments, providing the foodstuffs and equipment that a war demands of the economy.

The second phase of the cycle is usually a price inflation. Many of the goods produced in wartime are economic dead ends—the country has invested its time and money in products that are not reusable in the economy. After the war ends, there naturally arises a massive demand for civilian goods. The resulting postwar inflation may run for three to five years, reaching levels of inflation in the region of 5 to 6 percent, with bulges up to 12 percent or higher.

It is during this three-to-five-year period after a war that the judgment on runaway inflation should be made. If inflation does not reach double-digit proportions for longer than two consecutive years, the problems of runaway inflation should not be overemphasized. What happens instead is stage three, during which the currency of the country is brought down to a low enough level on the world markets to finance and stimulate an export boom. This export boom will usually carry the country into a major industrial supercycle upmove. During this stage, foreign countries buy the goods and services of the country and also invest heavily in its growth because of the low valuation of its currency in relationship to that of other countries.

This phase-three boom eventually reaches runaway proportions; it carries within it the seeds of its own destruction. After this, the fourth stage ushers in either depression or severe recession. During this period, the overextension of credit and excesses of the boom are atoned for. It is during this period that paper money and bloated credits used for business reach levels greatly extended in terms of real long-term value, and depression or severe recession are the correctives. Usually this stage planes down all the crests of stage three, which was the runaway upmove of the supercycle, and brings us back down to the beginning of another cycle.

This grand supercycle has existed throughout this century in the economic history of our country, and of the Dow averages. Stage one was World War I. This period lasted for about two years; following it, three years later in 1921, we had an inflation of very severe proportions. This raised the cost of commodities to extremely high levels and brought down the value of the US dollar on the world markets, which was stage two. Following the inflation of 1921, we entered stage three—the Dow Jones averages and the industrial boom soared to giddy new highs. The Dow averages rose from a level of 100 up to 380 in eight years. This era highlighted the extension of credit, the return of credibility of the dollar, and the return of confidence in the financial instruments of business. Faith returned to such an extent that we had a massive new-issue boom near the top (1928–29) and entry of the public in droves into the stock market.

Stage three ended with the swollen climax in the market and a collapse into the Great Depression from 1929 until 1932. This dismal depression was the herald for stage four, which exorcised the excesses of stage three and realigned the value of securities, commodities, and real estate at distressingly low prices.

The 1929 crash sent shock waves rippling through the stock market for decades afterward. With the crash over, the Dow Averages moved up with vigor from 1932 to 1937, as a modicum of confidence was restored. This market uptrend developed, ironically, during the worst period of the Depression—a classic case of the market moving ahead of the economy. This is because the stock market is more of a barometer than a thermometer. Thermometers record, but barometers project or foretell, and that is why the Dow has in most instances discounted the import of business news (by the time such news becomes public knowledge).

The easy-credit environment of the 1920s was over. Stocks could no longer be purchased on margin of only 10 percent. Business was conducted on such old-fashioned concepts as credit worthiness. Orders were paid for in advance, and bankers looked for collateral. Money was scarce. The volume during this period was created by fewer investors, those in sound financial condition, who sought seasoned stocks where the yields were high. Trading volume, even though the prices of the averages were half what they had been ten years previous, was sharply diminished, so that the value of transactions in this postcrash era fell. Investors generally were using assets salvaged from the erosion of depression, and only slowly rebuilding their resources for equity investment.

From 1932 until the early 1940s, stocks flowed back into the hands of wealthy long-term investors; it was a classic opportunity for buying stocks for pure investment value. The market was returning to undervaluation after an excessive speculative splurge. Shares in many companies were selling at book value or less. The dismal economic news, extensive press coverage of high unemployment, slow recovery, and impending war, had moved stocks out of the hands of weak, undercapitalized individuals into the hands of the wealthy investors resourceful enough to withstand adverse interim price swings and retain their positions for long-term investment growth on a grand scale.

The resurgent years of 1932 to 1942 found steep, precipitous breaks in the market followed by rallies and then again steep breaks. But the breaks during this period failed to penetrate the 1932 lows. In fact, the whole period was a slow assimilation of the excess supplies of stock—a period of base-building and reassessment of the country's potential future. The years following proved the 1932–42 phase to be a time of major opportunity; it is very important to realize that this period found the country in one of its most negative moods.

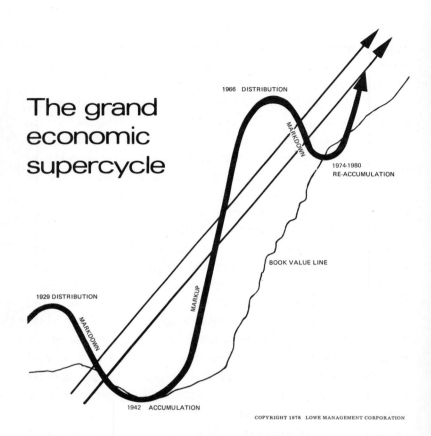

The grand economic supercycle

1966 DISTRIBUTION

MARKDOWN

1974-1980
RE-ACCUMULATION

BOOK VALUE LINE

1929 DISTRIBUTION

MARKDOWN

MARKUP

1942 ACCUMULATION

**Chart 1** The Grand Economic Supercycle: This four-stage rhythmic pattern begins when the Dow Averages are below book value. As can be seen from the chart, we are now bottoming and accelerating to the upside.

## The Cycle Repeats

With World War II, we again entered stage one of the grand economic supercycle. The industrial strength of this country was restored to normal levels, but the cost of war induced inflation. In the early 1950s, inflation again occurred three to five years after a war, and reached very high levels.

Stock prices were still low, especially compared with a decade later. With the Korean War past, the market began climbing at a steeper pace, generating one wave after another, bringing the Dow to new heights. This grand bull market was on its way to a new series of high plateaus. Every reaction witnessed in 1953 and 1957 and in 1962 was followed by a new all-time high. Stocks were snapped up as confident investors flocked back into the market.

Speculation was becoming more and more in vogue, and investing for dividend return was no longer the prime motivation. Investors sought the quick, exciting gains that come from fast upmovements of speculative stocks. Speculation became the dominant factor in investors' entry into the market. During this period, stocks broke away from their basic book values and commanded higher and higher prices in relation to their reported earnings. We were in a market that placed premiums on exciting stocks as people combed the lists for stocks that could double or even triple in relatively short spaces of time. The quest for capital gains became a way of life for middle America; the public came back into the market.

The whole ascent (stage three) had its most powerful upthrust within sixteen years between 1950 and 1966. This period witnessed the Dow climb from the 200 level as we entered the 1950s to the 1000 mark in February of 1966. What began as an investment move in the early fifties grew into a wild speculative climax in 1966, and played a final encore in 1968 with the new-issue speculative boom. This is a progression characteristic of all grand-scale bull markets.

Stage four of this supercycle never became a full depression but came in the form of three recessions: 1966, 1970, and 1974. Altogether these recessions eliminated most of the excesses of the post-World War II boom as in succession the Dow Jones defined a major bear market in 1966, a major bear market in 1970, and a major bear market in 1974.

What is interesting about these erosive downturns is that they were followed by animate realities on the upside. We are, in fact, still in this Yo-yo trading range, which has worn out the patience of millions of investors in much the same way that the 1929–32 Depression exiled investors from the market. What the 1929 bear market did in price, the 1966 grand-scale bear market has done in time. It has managed to remove the speculative zing from the market; although the average stocks have not come down 80 or 90 percent all at once as they did in 1929, in broad price terms, the majority of stocks today have been in equally erosive grand-scale bear markets. This has been due not only to speculative inertia in stocks, but also to high interest rates. In 1978–79, "prime" bonds yielding 8 to 10 percent replaced stocks in many portfolios.

## Stage Three Once Again?

The Viet Nam war became stage one of another economic supercycle. The war in Viet Nam cost trillions of dollars. This cost was predictably inflationary and motivated stage two during the early and mid-seventies, an important inflation again arriving approximately three to five years after the war reached its peak, during the Tet Offensive in 1968. During this stage two, gold soared on the world markets as the dollar sank to new lows. This is the stage from which we are now emerging. As we approach the 1980s, we are about to enter the explosive stage-three phase.

Stage three is the most powerful, profitable, and dynamic phase of the cycle. Many of the problems caused by stage two—the low valuation of the dollar, inflation, the energy crisis, very low levels of credibility and confidence—will evaporate. What we will witness once the grand bull market gets under way is a return to confidence in stocks, bonds, and our economic system in massive proportions. What we predict is that the Dow Jones Averages during this period will soar.

During this phase three, we will find an important change in the character of the news background through the media. Right now the public understanding of inflation is based on extrapolation of the diminished purchasing power of the dollar. The major fallacy in this understanding is based upon the national debt. Since 1949 the national debt has soared to all-time-high levels. This debt keeps growing year after year, as the government pursues a plan of deficit spending. This deficit spending (aggravated by Viet Nam) is the cause of the present inflation, and it will continue to be a definite ingredient in future inflation. This debt, however, has bought much of the industrial strength that this country has today.

In 1949, during the post-World War II period, we found that the national debt made some very important and substantial moves to the upside. It is now at all-time highs, and each year that we pursue a course of deficit spending this debt increases. What many of those concerned about the fall of the dollar today fail to realize is that the gross national product has far outpaced the movement of the national debt to the upside. This demonstrates that our national debt has paid for a good portion of today's economic growth. In coming years we will find that most of the investments made and financed by this debt will begin to show more and more productivity, as foreign countries purchase American goods and services. It is time to realize that the economic pendulum is now about to swing dramatically to the other end of the spectrum. Capitalism will flourish.

Today's inflation will give way, as it has in other periods, to a new grand-scale economic boom. This inflation is putting our economic system on the springboards to new all-time highs in productivity, growth, and profitability. This will broaden our tax base and balance our national budget. This will happen as soon as the dollar falls to a low enough level on the world markets to attract the buying of our goods and services on a broad scale.

At some time during each year from 1963 to 1979, the Dow Average has been in the 800 to 900 zone. This price range establishes a new base from which the supplies of stock may be conveyed from a generation of speculators to a new market generation of more resolute investors. In taking a grand bull market investment approach, it is important to determine, as precisely as possible, when this transition from one generation to the next is at hand.

We think that now is the time, after a series of recessions, when the US economy is poised to blossom anew. History is ready to repeat. As we enter the final decades of the twentieth century, we are due for one more grand bull market. It is important to remember that the beginning of a grand bull market starts at a time when most have forgotten how swiftly and powerfully market momentum can be

As can be seen from this chart, the market as represented by the Dow Jones Industrial Averages is undervalued on the basis of all three fundamental parameters: book value, earnings, and dividends. Here is a complete explanation of each of the three fundamental parameters for the Dow Averages:

■ **Earnings**   The Dow Jones price-to-earnings-ratio line is created by multiplying the earnings of the Dow Jones Averages by a factor of 9 and 18. Earnings undervaluation zone: When the Dow has a price-to-earnings ratio of 9 or less, the market is in a long-term area of accumulation. Earnings overvaluation zone: When the Dow has a price-to-earnings ratio of 18 or more, the Dow is in an area of distribution.

■ **Book Value**   Book value undervaluation zone: When the Dow sells below its book value, investors have an excellent opportunity to buy stocks at historically low prices. Book value overvaluation zone: When speculative fever moves prices to 2 times book value or greater, an excellent selling opportunity is created.

■ **Dividend Yield**   Dividend undervaluation zone: When the dividend yield on the Dow is 6 percent per year or greater, the Dow Averages are ripe for long-term dividend investors. Dividend overvaluation zone: When the dividend yield on the Dow Averages is 3 percent, the market has attracted a great speculative interest and has priced the Dow Averages too high for long-term investors seeking yield.

generated by incoming cyclical tidal waves of prosperity. The market is now positioning itself in such a way as to delude the great mass of investors; instead, far-seeing investors are accumulating the floating supplies of desirable company shares. This is exactly the position the market should be in for a massive move to the upside.

No two decades are the same. The accumulation in the seventies will generate a market that will cause overlooked fundamentals to be valued at much higher prices in the eighties. The present negative economic thinking gives capital-rich investors seeking dividend yield the opportunity to accumulate high-grade investment quality stocks under the cover of weakness, and to establish rewarding speculative positions at unusually low risks in the present-day market. The dividend-conscious market we are now in is also the kind that usually exists before major and substantial up-moves. The dividend market enables investors to buy stocks and hold on to them for years, while they are receiving high yields in relationship to historically low valuations of stock prices.

# PART TWO
## DOWBEATER
## METHODS

## 3

# How the Rich
# Get Richer!

## The East/West Investment Technique

The most certain way to protect your principal in the stock market is to invest only with the interest it earns. Too often investors attempt overnight riches, failing to realize that it is not the killing which makes for market success, but rather the compounding effects that a consistent investment strategy provides over a period of years. Windfall profits mean nothing unless they are maintained and maximized. Thus, applying conservative banking principles, speculating only with interest earned by one's investment program, in the long run yields an improved return on capital in a much more consistent fashion.

Many investors aim for a 50 to 100 percent return per

year on their investments. That is, for most, too high. In reality, a 10 to 20 percent return per year on capital is sufficient to compound even small amounts of money into a plump nest egg over the course of a decade as seen from the following table.

## Ten years compound gain

| At an annual percent gain of | $10,000 grows to ... | At an annual percent gain of | $10,000 grows to ... |
|---|---|---|---|
| 0% | $10,000 | 0% | $ 10,000 |
| 1% | 11,046 | + 10% | 25,937 |
| 2% | 12,190 | + 20% | 61,917 |
| 3% | 13,439 | + 30% | 137,858 |
| 4% | 14,802 | + 40% | 289,255 |
| 5% | 16,289 | + 50% | 576,650 |
| 6% | 17,908 | + 60% | 1,099,512 |
| 7% | 19,672 | + 70% | 2,015,994 |
| 8% | 21,589 | + 80% | 3,570,047 |
| 9% | 23,674 | + 90% | 6,131,066 |
| 10% | 25,937 | +100% | 10,240,000 |

In today's bond market, yields are the highest they have been for over a century. Consequently, now is almost an ideal time to start a program of investing with principal, and speculating with interest.

## Building the East Pool

The formula for speculating with interest is the basic procedure on which the super fortunes amassed in this country have been built and enhanced. The simple reason the rich get richer is that they can speculate with their interest income. Here's how *you* can use the same approach.

First of all, one must build a pool of capital consisting of ultraconservative investments. This pool of capital, which we'll call the East Pool, should be invested in bonds, savings accounts, and/or short-term paper. These conservative media give an investor both strong basic capital and sufficient income to keep positioned to make large returns on his more aggressive investments, while keeping his principal intact. The investor can survive a wrong decision or a series of wrong decisions because he risks only the interest on his principal, not the basic fund itself. Such a strategy eliminates that large gray area of investing in which investments seem to offer both a conservative return and the possibility for dynamic growth. This paradoxical goal often proves unattainable, and may indeed lead to serious losses.

The aggregate yield from the East Pool should be between 6 and 10 percent, depending upon the interest-rate structure that prevails.

A penny saved is a penny earned. Therefore, the first and foremost investment every "investor" should make in structuring an East Pool should be in a regular passbook savings account. A savings account provides the investor with instant availability to his money without market depreciation and a solid building block for financial success. A savings account should be the bedrock foundation of your financial pyramid. As history has proven, a solid foundation may ultimately translate into large speculative gains.

A second vehicle for capital deployment in the East Pool is the certificate of deposit, taken on an annual basis. These notes provide the investor with slightly better yield than a savings account, and they add to the diversification of the East Pool.

Further, we recommend investing in Treasury Bills and other short-term paper. It is generally wise to buy T Bills with a six-month duration or less. That way you are not subject to interest rate changes. The best municipal bonds to buy are those that will come due in the next three to five years. These offer a high tax-free yield, plus a return of principal as they come due. This short-term approach to municipal bonds gives the investor tax-free yield, with protection against fluctuations in the money market. These diversified East Pool investments give the investor a solid base that can support entry into the more speculative and, hopefully, more profitable investments. In other words, this program will generate income to continually fuel a speculative and aggressive West Pool program.

## Building the West Pool

The purpose of the West Pool is to use the interest earned on principal in such a way that one dollar does the work of ten to twenty. The selection of the trading vehicles to be used in the West Pool must, therefore, be made with particular discrimination. First of all, West Pool investments must be oriented toward high leverage. While the reason for investing in the East Pool was to generate and assure a conservative return, in the West Pool investments are made ultra-aggressively, in high-risk vehicles to achieve capital gains.

However, once positions in the West Pool are closed out,

profits revert to and are reinvested in the East Pool. This assures that capital deployed in the West Pool is put to work in a program designed ultimately to enhance the capital in the East Pool. As long as the East Pool is fueled with the profits from the West, the capital resources invested will continue to grow and will thus continually build a broader interest base for the investor. Such a program assures that dynamic speculative gains that may occur in the market are not frittered away but rather compounded, by recycling the aggressive speculative profits back into the conservative pool.

As long as the investor limits his speculative funds to interest received, he's in a strong and relatively hazard-free position. Using the East and West Pools, the investor has working for him both a defensive and an offensive strategy in his money-management program. He is able to survive speculative misfires; and even more important, he is always able to keep his basic investment capital intact.

By far the best kind of investments in the West Pool are low- and ultra-low-priced stocks. These offer the investor the potential for large speculative gains in the coming years. Now, and in the past few years, low-priced stocks have been relatively dormant. There has been little public sponsorship of these stocks. In fact, many are selling substantially below their historic levels, and in many instances below book value. This could mean that many may be poised to swing into explosive moves in the 1980s.

The reason we believe this will happen is that many of these low-priced companies are in a stronger position now than they have ever been before. These companies are in a powerful position to leverage their capital through the technological advances they are making. In addition, these companies are capable of increasing their sales dramatically because of their small size relative to the industries they are in. Theoretically, it is much easier for a company to double its sales from a $25 million sales base than it is for General Motors with its sales base in the billions, as it already represents 64 percent of this country's automobile industry.

These lesser companies offer high leverage and visible potential for exponential gains in the coming decade. There have been low periods in the history of the stock market which offered such excellent opportunities, at such attractive prices. There is no doubt that some of these shares will gain between 500 and 1000 percent in market value, once the speculative fever returns to Wall Street. This fertile field for investment is indeed likely to spawn the companies that will be the new IBM, the new Xerox, or the new Polaroid.

Right now, most investors are asleep. We are emerging from a period of deep gloom in the stock market, a period that put maximum pressures on low-priced stocks. However, this period of gloom and lack of confidence is an ideal opportunity to build a diversified West Pool of low-priced stocks. The West Pool ought to consist of between seven and ten issues selling between $2 and $5 a share. It's from these price levels that exponential gains are most likely. This probability of superperformance gains is further enhanced by the total disillusionment the public has with today's stock market.

When the Dow Jones Averages climb to new all-time highs the public will race to get back into the market. The result will be an overnight musical chairs scramble among investors seeking to buy shares of low-priced stocks. Once this speculative fever begins, it will run rampant and persist for many years. Right now, while these stocks are at such low points of valuation, is the ideal time to purchase them—using, of course, the dividends and interest earned in the East Pool.

There are many possible variations of the basic East and West Pool Investment Plan. The plan is obviously flexible. However, regardless of the modifications made and the different trading vehicles employed in either the East or the West Pools, make certain to keep the East Pool ultra-conservative and the West Pool ultra-aggressive. In this way you'll be protected against the inevitable shifts that occur in the market.

## The West Pool Options Strategy

The advent of the options market has created a new investment wave. If this wave repeats the pattern of all other investment waves, most investors will not prosper but will, in the long run, lose money. This is because the options market creates the most dynamic leverage that the stock market has ever offered. Unfortunately, investors will find that leverage is a double-edged sword—the profits earned are as easily lost again, and as quickly. All too often, investors find themselves overinvested in a highly leveraged situation. In many cases, the leverage that is offered in the options markets is greater than the leverages that could be attained in the days before the 1929 crash, when stocks could be purchased at 10 percent margin. Today, an investor can achieve the same leverage power·of 1 to 10 through the purchase of options, and the purchaser of options has a limited downside risk, as he can only lose his initial nominal investment. This makes the option market a dynamic, potentially profitable money-management tool. With the leverage that is available in the options market, investors can make one dollar do the work of twenty. This means that an investor with a one-thousand-dollar investment can control twenty thousand dollars worth of stocks for certain periods of time, usually six to nine months. With such powerful leverage there is no reason for an investor to speculate with any more than the interest he's earned on his capital.

Nevertheless, it is essential to follow a few simple guidelines when speculating in options. The first is that, as already stated, options should never be bought with capital other than the interest capital that has been earned from principal. The second guideline to remember is that options above $3 should usually not be purchased. There is no reason to lose more than 3 to 5 points in any speculation, and much of the leverage on an option investment is lost when an option is above $3. Profits realized in the options market should be converted to cash on a quarterly basis and reinvested in the East Pool. Finally, as there are often cases where options positions double in value literally overnight, when this happens half an option investor's own position should be liquidated and the original capital recaptured.

The options market is not for beginners. The great volatility that exists within the options market exists only for the benefit—that is, the profit—of a few. Careful study and a great amount of time must be devoted before any option position is taken. If these guidelines are followed, the East/West Options Strategy is ideal for speculative purposes.

## The West Pool New-Issue Strategy

We are now entering a new phase in American economic history, which will require a huge influx of speculative capital. As the market explodes on the upside, there will again (as in the 1950s and 1960s) be hundreds of small, innovative companies offering their shares to the public for the first time. These companies may hold promise of new breakthroughs in technology, and some may become notably profitable in the 1980s. Although investing in these companies requires a carefully acquired and thorough understanding of the background of each company and the industry it is a part of before one invests, the gains from this early-entry speculation can be enormous.

So, also, can the pitfalls. One need only examine the 1962 or, for that matter, the 1968 new-issue boom. Ultimately both produced far more losers than gainers. On the other hand, there is no company on the exchanges today that was not at one time either a new issue or a spinoff of a company that was a new issue. Thus, the third trading vehicle recommended to complete the West Pool Investment Program is carefully selected new issues. Chart 2, on page 36, summarizes the complete East-West Investment Technique.

Keep in mind the fact that the technological growth of the American economy has come largely from those who are willing to speculate. Every idea, every production, every invention was someone's speculation at one point. Successful speculation requires both a vision of the future and the courage and funds to take action before an opportunity is lost. With any speculation there is, of course, no guarantee that profits will be made. The goal of any speculation, and

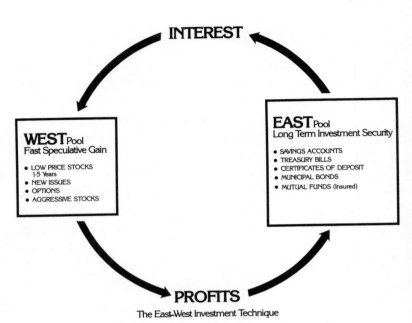

INTEREST

**WEST**Pool
Fast Speculative Gain

- LOW PRICE STOCKS
  1-5 Years
- NEW ISSUES
- OPTIONS
- AGGRESSIVE STOCKS

**EAST**Pool
Long Term Investment Security

- SAVINGS ACCOUNTS
- TREASURY BILLS
- CERTIFICATES OF DEPOSIT
- MUNICIPAL BONDS
- MUTUAL FUNDS (Insured)

PROFITS

The East-West Investment Technique

**Chart 2**  The East-West Investment Technique: The ultra-conservative East Pool investment interest fuels the ultra-aggressive West Pool; profits from the West Pool then recycle back to the East Pool. This creates a greater base of principal, which then returns even larger amounts of interest to the West Pool. In years when West Pool speculations are unsuccessful, the East Pool principal remains intact.

this includes speculation in the options market, is to find probably one situation out of three that will result in phenomenal rewards. There are no guarantees in any speculation except the guarantee that you can give yourself: Speculate only with interest from a fund composed of conservative assured-income securities, diversified both as to type and maturity.

# 4

# The Two Main Methods of
# Security Analysis

## How to Discover Which Stocks to Buy

Over the years the procedures for security evaluation have become divided into two major categories: fundamental and technical analysis. The fundamental method is based on the theory that, over a period of time, stock prices are the slaves of earning power. The market fundamentalist gathers basic statistical data about an industry and the companies within it, and from these data he rates the relative attractiveness of particular issues at their current prices. He attempts to determine whether a stock is a sound issue and if it will go higher or lower, by virtue of available statistical information.

The material (which must be constantly reviewed and updated) considered by fundamental analysts includes a company's past and current earnings; profit margins; price/

earnings multiples; earnings rates on invested capital; stockholders' equity (book value); capitalization ratio of debt to equity; current asset/liability ratios; rates of growth; taxation; cash flow; dividend policy; labor relations; expenditures for research; international business, merger, or acquisition prospects; new products, goods, or services. Market acceptance of products and reputation for quality are also important factors.

Overall fundamental factors would include the trends in a particular industry, interest and inflation rates, monetary stability, government regulation, environmental problems, and the indicated state and direction of the entire economy —recession, boom, or stagnation. Of these, interest rates are among the most important determinants because when interest rates are low, corporations can borrow economically, and individuals can borrow to buy stock. Any steep increase in interest rates has almost always depressed stock prices.

Finally, the fundamentalist will make value determinations on the quality and effectiveness of corporate managements. Are they stodgy, progressive, cost-conscious, imaginative, innovative, young, promotion-minded, or ingrown? Above all, do they own a lot of stock in the company themselves?

An ongoing coverage of the above items, developed by a constant flow of information contained in corporation interim and annual reports, provides the fundamentalist with what he needs to determine the desirability of a particular security. The conclusions are based on the knowledge, the experience, and the judgment of each analyst. Even with identical data, however, opposite opinions may develop; unanimous approval as to the desirability of a stock is not a frequent phenomenon among fundamentalists.

By far the greatest numbers of security analysts use the fundamental method. They are less concerned with price swings and the level and direction of the market than in significant potentials for the rise or fall in corporate earnings or dividends. Indeed, many fundamentalists believe that there is no reliable method for predicting market directions in advance. Since their research can dig up such exciting winners as Xerox, IBM, Diagnostic Data, Houston Oil & Minerals, Twentieth Century Fox, Dome Mines, 3M, and Houston Natural Gas, they also believe that outstanding earning power can and will be generously rewarded even in dull markets.

Many other market professionals, however, contend that appraisal of stocks strictly on a fundamental basis is incomplete. They insist that the market is a dual phenomenon—psychological as well as logical—and that a changing psychological climate in Wall Street can affect the prices of securities quite as powerfully as changes in earnings or dividends. Some have suggested that under "average" economic conditions the controlling factors are 70 percent fundamental or logical and 30 percent cyclical or psychological, but in the extremes of a boom or recession the ratios change drastically; the cyclical market action or response of individuals then becomes the controlling factor in influencing decisions to buy or sell to the extent of 70 percent or more.

## Technical Analysis

The second major procedure in security appraisal, and more specifically directed toward market timing, is technical analysis. This system arrives at stock valuations by studying the day-by-day performance of individual stocks and the market as a whole; by carefully recording and charting the daily volumes of trading and price movements in issues. Technical analysis attempts to discern future price trends from past performance of active stocks, or from barometers such as the DJIA. The technician insists that in making determinations about a stock, a perception or reading of the prevailing trend in the market as a whole and in the particular issue is a more reliable instant guide than reported or estimated earnings or dividends.

Often markets go up or down quite dramatically, without any significant change in fundamental values. Prices are arrived at by a sort of mass movement, psychologically induced, of public money into or out of the market. The success of landings on the moon could not be evaluated by statistics or on profit-and-loss statements, but it did give great market stimulus to scientific equities. When President Kennedy died, the market sank; but it bounded back up a few weeks later when the grief of an emotion-struck nation had subsided. These sudden floods of investment capital into, and out of, the market become evident when: (1) the daily trading volume on major exchanges increases noticeably; (2) increase in volume is accompanied by new "highs" in popular issues. Conversely, when volume increases inordinately on the down side, in general, the sale of stocks is indicated and a further price decline may be expected.

To record and analyze these price and volume data, charts are essential to the technician. There are two principal kinds: *bar charts* and *point and figure charts*.

The popular bar chart may cover transactions for a day, a week, a month, a quarter, or a year. Customarily the horizontal scale on the chart, running from left to right, will represent the time scale in the period charted; the vertical scale will reflect price changes.

Plotting such a chart has become fairly standardized. One connects the day's high and the day's low by a vertical line; the closing price is indicated by a very short horizontal line crossing the vertical one. You plot in the same data for each succeeding trading day, and shortly you have a chart that reveals a trend—which is what you're looking for.

Volume is usually shown on a special scale running along the bottom of the page; and many charts also carry notes at the bottom indicating when a stock sells ex dividend or ex rights or pays an extra or stock dividend.

If you are a neat person with a mathematical turn of mind, you can plot and keep up these charts yourself. Most people, however, prefer to view such charts published along with many research studies on individual stocks in financial journals or as mailed regularly to subscribers of such services as Trendline, Mansfield, M. C. Horsey, Value Line, Standard & Poor's, etc.

These charts, properly constructed, provide valuable information. First, they reveal what people were willing to pay or accept for a given stock on any day. This price represents the ultimate value of a stock—what it will fetch in the marketplace. Emotion, caprice, or mass psychology, rather than reason, may have influenced the prices recorded; but prices do not lie. The chart reveals the "blooodless verdict of the marketplace." Never mind earnings prospects, glamour, or sponsorship—a stock is worth, on a particular day, no more and no less than what it sold for!

A succession of these weekly or monthly charts, according to technicians, should reveal a dominant directional

# LTV CORPORATION (THE)

nyse
LTV

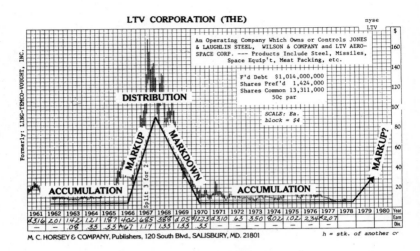

An Operating Company Which Owns or Controls JONES & LAUGHLIN STEEL, WILSON & COMPANY and LTV AERO-SPACE CORP. --- Products Include Steel, Missiles, Space Equip't, Meat Packing, etc.

F'd Debt $1,014,000,000
Shares Pref'd 1,424,000
Shares Common 13,311,000
50c par

SCALE: Ea. block = $4

Formerly: LING-TEMCO-VOUGHT, INC.

DISTRIBUTION

MARKUP  MARKDOWN  Split 3 for 2

ACCUMULATION   ACCUMULATION   MARKUP?

| | 1961 | 1962 | 1963 | 1964 | 1965 | 1966 | 1967 | 1968 | 1969 | 1970 | 1971 | 1972 | 1973 | 1974 | 1975 | 1976 | 1977 | 1978 | 1979 | 1980 | Year |
|---|---|---|---|---|---|---|---|---|---|---|---|---|---|---|---|---|---|---|---|---|---|
| | 2316 | 201 | 142 | 121 | 187 | 402 | 685 | 388 | d05 | d273 | d310 | 63 | 350 | 802 | 102 | 234 | 207 | | | | Earn |
| | — | — | .08 | .35 | .33 | .67 | 1.17 | 1.33 | 1.33 | .35 | — | — | — | — | — | — | — | | | | Div. |

M. C. HORSEY & COMPANY, Publishers, 120 South Blvd., SALISBURY, MD. 21801

h = stk. of another cr

**Chart 3** Bar chart of LTV: This shows the potential upmove of LTV from its years of accumulation below $20 per share. Accumulation is part of a four-stage cycle clearly identifiable on long-term monthly charts, the stages being:

1. Accumulation—during this time, long-term investors take their positions.
2. Markup—as a result of the sharp tightening of supplies, during accumulation, prices move up.
3. Distribution—the farsightedness of the investor during the accumulation stage pays off. The news is out and the public buys and the professionals sell.
4. Markdown—Distribution is now over. Price weakness sets in. The public has just bought the "good news" and the stock promptly sells off. With public now in, who is left to buy? The results: markdown in prices.

Will LTV now repeat this cycle again? (See Lazarus Securities.)

trend. An upthrust may be motivated by net earnings rising significantly in each quarter, or by a general market confidence pushing up all stocks—the weak along with the

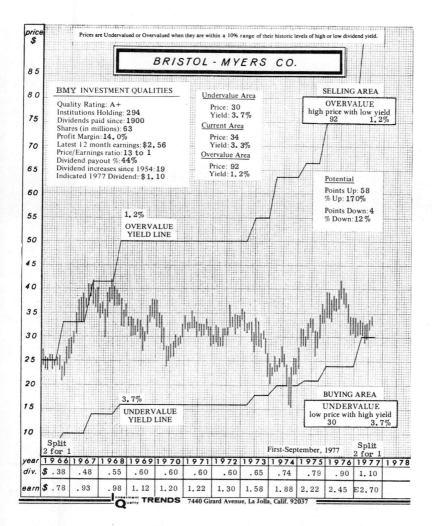

Prices are Undervalued or Overvalued when they are within a 10% range of their historic levels of high or low dividend yield.

## BRISTOL - MYERS CO.

**BMY INVESTMENT QUALITIES**

Quality Rating: A+
Institutions Holding: 294
Dividends paid since: 1900
Shares (in millions): 63
Profit Margin: 14. 0%
Latest 12 month earnings: $2. 56
Price/Earnings ratio: 13 to 1
Dividend payout %: 44%
Dividend increases since 1954: 19
Indicated 1977 Dividend: $1. 10

Undervalue Area
Price: 30
Yield: 3. 7%

Current Area
Price: 34
Yield: 3. 3%

Overvalue Area
Price: 92
Yield: 1. 2%

SELLING AREA

OVERVALUE
high price with low yield
92          1. 2%

Potential

Points Up: 58
% Up: 170%

Points Down: 4
% Down: 12%

1. 2%
OVERVALUE
YIELD LINE

3. 7%
UNDERVALUE
YIELD LINE

BUYING AREA

UNDERVALUE
low price with high yield
30          3. 7%

Split
2 for 1

First-September, 1977

Split
2 for 1

| year | 1966 | 1967 | 1968 | 1969 | 1970 | 1971 | 1972 | 1973 | 1974 | 1975 | 1976 | 1977 | 1978 |
|------|------|------|------|------|------|------|------|------|------|------|------|------|------|
| div. $ | .38 | .48 | .55 | .60 | .60 | .60 | .60 | .65 | .74 | .79 | .90 | 1.10 | |
| earn $ | .78 | .93 | .98 | 1.12 | 1.20 | 1.22 | 1.30 | 1.58 | 1.88 | 2.22 | 2.45 | E2.70 | |

Investment Quality **TRENDS**   7440 Girard Avenue, La Jolla, Calif. 92037

**Chart 4**   Bar chart of Bristol Myers: This identifies the relationship of stock price with the fundamental parameter of dividend yield. Notice how the price finds support near its 3.7 percent historical dividend band. This very informative chart shows Bristol Myers to be undervalued.

strong. A downturn may sensitively reflect a decline in investor confidence.

The preceding charts portray graphically the kinds of messages bar charts portray: the four seasons of price movement of LTV (an interesting speculation); and the price value relationships of Bristol Myers Co. (an excellent high quality investment).

We can't begin to cover here all the nuances of barchart analysis, such as reversals, breakouts, boxes, rectangles, head-and-shoulder formations, consolidations, etc. For real professional guidance in this area we urge you to get a book called *Technical Analysis*, by Edwards and Magee. This book can give you a basic course on the subject of charts and help you use the technical approach to detect peaks and valleys and identify patterns of supply and demand in individual stocks that may project the prices they may reach a few months hence.

## Point and Figure Charts

A less common, more sophisticated chart used by technicians is called the *point and figure chart,* used to reflect trading value. Here a uniform chart paper is used, with each box or square representing a unit of price. Customarily each square will represent a one-point move in the price of a stock (in shares selling below 20, each box may represent only half a point). Price changes, in order to show on the chart, must cover at least three squares, up or down. If an issue continues to trade within a very narrow range, day after day, then the chart will remain unchanged. Only if the stock "breaks out" either up or down will changes actually get plotted. The letter X is customarily used to denote up moves, and O for downs. Trendlines are not drawn until a bullish or bearish formation has appeared. Then a trendline will be constructed at an angle of 45 degrees. Shares are thought to be in a buying range when transactions are above the trendline, and in a selling phase when transactions take place below.

Point and figure charts ignore the time factor, since they only reflect trading volume. Such charts may be "flat" for a week or ten days at a time, and then zig and zag like an oscilloscope within one or two active trading days. P & F charts simply record changes in price, and in this way describe those demand/supply factors affecting a particular stock that may elevate or lower its quotations. The theory is that if demand is strong (more insistent than supply) a stock will continue to go up until supply (selling pressure) emerges.

The technical theory postulates a series of market waves; and the objective is to divine by charts and their interpretation the length, height, and duration of these waves. There is evidence that institutional investors, particularly since the market debacle of 1974, have been placing increasing confidence in the prognostications of their technical analysts.

Substantial exchange firms employ technical analysts along with a battery of the fundamental variety. Among the technical virtuosi are Donald Hahn of Becker Securities Co., Chicago; Robert Farrell of Merrill Lynch; Stanley Berge of Tucker Anthony, R. L. Day; Ned Davis of J. C. Bradford, Nashville; and Gail Dudack of Pershing & Co. Many metropolitan banks have staff technicians also.

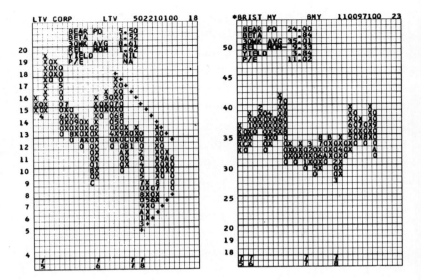

**Charts 5 and 6** Point and figure charts of LTV and Bristol Myers: These show the interacting forces of supply (Os) and demand (Xs) for these two stocks. These charts not only show trend action, but also show potential price objectives through a counting formula. This count shows, during areas of accumulation or distribution, the approximate potential price moves from these zones. (*Charts courtesy of Chartcraft, Inc., Larchmont, N.Y.*)

Some of these technicians have gained considerable acclaim for their accuracy in calling market turns. Aided by carefully manicured charts and precise graphs, these market "pros" have frequently accurately predicted the impact of mass psychology and its magnetic influence on security prices.

Charts identify the flow of money in and out of the market and record market volume, volatility, short sales, and the relative desirability of competing forms of investments, particularly bonds. The growth in money rates is also factored in by many technicians. They contend that the amount of money in circulation has a vital bearing on that portion that flows into securities. Declines in money supply have in recent times, quite predictably, depressed P/E multiples for stocks.

Technical analysis is a useful tool and a powerful cross-check on fundamental analysis. In the selection of Dow-beaters the fudamentals must be right—strong balance sheets, upcurves in earnings, high profit margins and high return on equity, etc., but we also like to look at a current bar chart on the issue and the Dow averages. If these, too, are "uptick" we have welcome confirmation that the security researched is favorably positioned for current purchase. Further, we'd think twice about a recommendation if a bar or P & F chart of a stock were strongly adverse. We might still favor the stock but await a more propitious time for its purchase.

Neither basic method of stock analysis is an answer in itself. By combining the strengths of both methods new dimensions of portfolio strategy unfold. The following Dow-beater methods show how.

# 5

# The Eclipse Method
# of Investing

## A Deductive Stock-Market Timing Approach

The essential problem for any investor is identifying the times opportune for entering the bull markets while still retaining the flexibility to adjust investments during those negative periods of blind spots in the market, when stock prices erode due to bear markets or sharp panic breaks. The *eclipse method* of investing presents one way of solving this problem. The eclipse method of investing buys in the market's dark periods and sells when the crowd regains confidence, and especially overconfidence, in the market. These dark periods occur during stock-market declines, when the light of reason is blocked from the shortsighted mass-investing public.

Lowry's Reports, Inc. is probably the best guide to eclipse investing. For the past forty years, Lowry's Reports have been giving specific buy-and-sell advice, based on the supply-demand relationship of the entire market.

The Lowry method is based on the theory that stock prices are governed by the law of supply and demand. In other words, when there are more buyers than sellers, stocks go up. When there are more sellers than buyers, stocks go down. In order to detect the extent of buying or selling pressure, Lowry's measures both the volume (number of shares) of stocks traded daily and the total amount of gains and losses of those traded. These measurements are then plugged into a formula that, when computed, gives a buy or sell signal (Leisner, p. 67).

According to the Lowry theory,

Stocks only do two things: Their prices fluctuate Up and Down; their Trading volume increases and decreases. That is all they ever do! Thus, the action of the entire market, which includes the combined actions of insiders, professionals, specialists, mutual funds, tape readers, short sellers, fundamentalists, chartists, bulls and bears, as well as the "public" and odd-lotters, can be reduced to simply 4 basic totals:

1. Total GAINS for all round-lot (100 shares) stocks closing higher than the previous day's close.
2. The total VOLUME of transactions for stocks registering gains.
3. Total LOSSES for stocks closing lower than the previous day's close, and—
4. The total VOLUME for declining stocks (Lowry's Reports, Inc., p. 3).

An examination of the results achieved with the Lowry

method reveals impressive performance. One recent study at the Finance Department of the Wharton School of Finance and Commerce indicates:

> The Lowry method of technical analysis, which utilizes only past price and volume data, led to returns of more than double those achieved by naive buy-and-hold investment programs. In addition, this performance was achieved in the face of very stringent operational limitations over a number of different time periods extending as far back as 25 years. This, of course, is an apparent contradiction of both the Efficient Markets and Random Walk theories (Roebuck and Roebuck, p. 24).

According to Paul Desmond, president of Lowry's, they have called the market moves in much the same way as a barometer predicts rain—not every time that the barometer says rain has it rained, but there has never been a time when it rained that the barometer *didn't* say rain. In other words, Lowry's method has called many market moves that didn't materialize, but there has never been a market move of major importance that was not foreseen by the Lowry's service. Obviously, such an indicator has great profit potential for the investor. It is no wonder that some 85 percent of Lowry's readers are professionals and that Lowry's is one of the most respected market services available today.

Lowry's method is particularly effective when coupled with the trading of mutual funds. When mutual funds are the trading vehicle and one is using Lowry's buy and sell signals, the door is opened to exponential possibilities of compounding. The performance of mutual funds is generally good to excellent during grand-scale bull markets. During sideways or eroding markets, mutual funds' performance is generally mediocre to poor. This is because mutual funds are structured to analyzing companies and industries but not the important and broad movements in the stock market. This is where Lowry's comes in: using Lowry's for the market timing, and mutual funds for the selection of individual industries and stocks, the investor has a complete investment program working for his advantage. In addition, the costs of trading no-load mutual funds is minimal. Usually these funds charge management fees of less than 1½ percent per year. Shown in Table I is a hypothetical performance summary of the Lowry conversion program applied to twenty-two of the largest no-load funds. In every case the Lowry conversion approach outperformed each fund and outperformed the Dow over the ten-year period.

As Paul Desmond explains it:

Mutual funds are a $47 billion industry, and with the liquidity requirements that go along with that industry, we could see where we could be fully invested in growth securities during periods of advance. Then, when we perceived the market decline, we could immediately liquidate within a matter of hours, go into a money market fund, a totally defensive vehicle, and wait for a new buy signal . . . and for almost no cost at all. Even with a load fund, once you pay your initial entrance fee, then you can stay within that family of funds and rotate back and forth indefinitely, permanently, as long as that option is available. It might be open for the next 25 or 50 years for a $5 fee for each transaction.

Now, to be able to roll a million or two or ten million dollars back and forth for $5 is no load. [No-load funds have no sales or commission charges.] IT IS NO LOAD. And in addition to the speed that you have, you have consistency. The mutual funds have a tremendous advantage over com-

# Table 1  Ten-year performance summary

(January 1, 1968 DJIA at 906.84 through December 30, 1977 DJIA at 831.57)
Assumed Investment: $1,000,000 on 1/1/68

| Fund | Buy/Hold | Annualized % Return Compounded | Lowry Conversion Program | Annualized % Return Compounded |
| --- | --- | --- | --- | --- |
| Amer. Gen. Cap. Growth | 572,000 | −5.4% | 2,005,892 | 7.2% |
| Broad Street | 1,783,293 | 6.0% | 3,462,425 | 13.3% |
| Chemical Fund | 1,298,875 | 2.7% | 2,300,000 | 8.7% |
| Colonial Growth | 725,689 | −3.2% | 2,315,169 | 8.7% |
| Comstock Fund | 1,277,000 | 2.5% | 2,870,786 | 11.1% |
| Dreyfus Fund | 1,237,342 | 2.2% | 2,413,944 | 9.2% |
| Enterprise Fund | 814,870 | −2.0% | 2,703,499 | 10.5% |
| Financial Ind. Income | 2,411,108 | 9.2% | 3,559,950 | 13.5% |
| Financial Ind. Fund | 1,472,029 | 4.0% | 2,393,523 | 9.1% |
| Invest. Co. of Amer. | 1,670,184 | 5.3% | 2,745,190 | 10.6% |
| Keystone S-3 Fund | 1,143,576 | 1.4% | 2,739,588 | 10.6% |
| Keystone S-4 Fund | 690,019 | −3.6% | 2,808,202 | 10.9% |
| Mass. Inv. Trust | 1,200,000 | 1.9% | 1,980,810 | 7.1% |
| National Investors | 1,282,239 | 2.5% | 3,126,456 | 12.1% |
| National Stock | 1,721,554 | 5.6% | 2,866,737 | 11.1% |
| Oppenheimer A.I.M.* | 1,322,690 | 3.6% | 2,295,953 | 10.9% |
| Oppenheimer Fund | 996,675 | −0.1% | 2,618,457 | 10.1% |
| Oppenheimer Time** | 921,885 | −0.7% | 2,000,744 | 12.3% |
| Pennsylvania Mutual | 664,514 | −4.1% | 6,154,627 | 18.3% |
| Putnam Investors | 1,678,479 | 5.3% | 2,499,144 | 9.6% |
| Putnam Growth | 1,399,509 | 3.4% | 2,409,130 | 9.2% |
| Windsor Fund | 2,096,427 | 7.7% | 3,292,037 | 12.7% |

## RECAP OF TEN-YEAR PERFORMANCE

| Investment Approach | Annualized % Return Compounded |
| --- | --- |
| Average Buy and Hold Program outlined above | 2.6% |
| "Indexing"—Standard & Poor's 500 Stock Index | 2.8% |
| Average Lowry Conversion Program outlined above | 10.9% |

* from 1/1/70
** from 1/1/72

mon stocks in that you can actually know with a very, very high degree of certainty before a market bottom occurs what you're going to want to be invested in. With common stocks, you just can't do that (Desmond, p. 13).

Using the Lowry buy and sell advice, the eclipse method of investing works as follows: Buy mutual funds holding high-quality stocks when Lowry's gives a buy signal; buy a mutual money market fund when Lowry's gives a sell signal. In this way an investor can participate profitably in the market's major upmoves while simultaneously being in a high cash position during stock-market setbacks.

Today most of the major mutual funds, such as Keystone, Oppenheimer, and Fidelity, have programs in which an investor can switch from cash funds into stock funds and back for a nominal fee. Thus, the investor can take maximum advantage of different management strategies to suit his particular needs of the moment. This allows the investor to switch within the same family of funds into the fund that gives him the best positions suited for the type of market environment at the specific time.

One of the foremost aspects of any successful market plan is a method of systematically cutting losses. The eclipse method of investing, using the Lowry buy signal, has preset criteria for identifying when supply is greater than demand and, consequently, when the position should be liquidated. This keeps the investor from the kind of losses that cripple his portfolio to the point of inaction. The concept of buying and selling mutual funds in accordance with the Lowry's buy and sell signals has evolved over many years. The idea of switching from one fund to the next according to a preset plan eliminates a great deal of the anxiety that accompanies investing.

Another problem that most investors have is finding a broadly diversified group of stocks that outperform the general market, as measured by the Dow Jones Industrial Averages. The eclipse investment method using Lowry's approach to buying and selling mutual funds builds capital appreciation through the power of compounding. For example, using Lowry's approach from 1950 to 1975 with the Keystone funds as the investment vehicle, the investor would have realized 23 percent a year compounded. These hypothetical results are far superior to the results achieved if an investor bought IBM stock in 1950 and held it until 1975, reinvesting all his dividends and keeping all his shares after stock splits. IBM, one of the greatest growth stocks of the post-World War II period, grew at a mere 17 percent per year compounded.

In addition, the Lowry organization manages its own unique open-end mutual fund and specialized managed account program. The Lowry Fund does not invest in common stocks, only in the shares of other mutual funds, as previously mentioned. In essence,

It is, as the industry men say, a "fund of funds" for these reasons:
1. Diversification—Since each mutual fund typically owns a large number of stocks, purchase by Lowry of mutual funds' shares makes each Lowry share represent many.
2. Liquidity—Unlike the direct purchase of individual stocks, shares in any one mutual fund can be bought or sold without causing stock prices to signifiicantly rise or fall.
3. Timing—Lowry can move in or out of the stock market quickly because mutual funds generally must redeem their shares from investors at net asset value (which is

typically close to the mutual fund share sales price) by the day after the "sell" order is received.

4. Cost of transactions—Some mutual funds charge little or no commission to buy or sell under certain conditions and allow investors to switch related funds at no charge. This is particularly important to Lowry when it can transfer in or out of family fund members specializing in highly liquid investments like Treasury bills (Peters, Section H, p. 1).

Insurance is available on the fund for a nominal fee if you hold the fund for ten years or longer; this guarantees to return your original principal.

The primary purpose of the Lowry Fund is to capitalize on the positive movements in the stock market and stay liquid during the negative periods. It is a professionally managed program that is broadly diversified through its purchase of mutual funds. The program has several built-in advantages as well: The investor's capital is managed by professionals. Once a position is taken in the mutual fund market, you have acquired a team of analysts and portfolio managers who work together to build a portfolio program designed for maximum growth and minimum risk. They analyze and assess the future earnings prospects of individual companies, their industries, and their positions in the economy. As it is rare for the fund to have more than 10 percent of its assets in any one particular company, the investor is protected against having all of his eggs in one basket. What often happens to an individual investor is that he becomes too concentrated in one stock, and a short-term, unexpected news announcement disbalances an investment program that took years of planning.

If investment funds are in a professionally managed Lowry portfolio, an investor can participate in market swings while staying on the sidelines with cash to reinvest profits when the market is lower. Moreover, losses are kept to an absolute minimum, since the mutual funds being traded are no load. The results are dramatic—considering what a conservatively based strategy this is. A hypothetical investor could have turned a $100,000 initial investment into $3,666,794 between January 1, 1960 and September 16, 1975 using such an approach—buying the Oppenheimer fund during Lowry's buy signals, for example, and staying in money market funds during Lowry's sell signals.

The stock market in the past fifteen-year period has been a broadly churning, sideways market. It has seen many fads come and go, the result of the short-term characteristics of sponsorship occurring during a market that is basically tremulous and in a period of reconsolidation. During these last fifteen years few investment philosophies have withstood the test of time. The Lowry approach combines many of the advantages of those investment philosophies which have performed the best over this period, plus having many advantages that are uniquely its own.

It is recommended that those who would like to use the Lowry approach study its method and its track record over the past forty years. Of course, there are no guarantees that the Lowry method will perform as well in the future as it has in the past. There could be several years during which the Lowry method could fail to produce substantial gains for the investor. But careful study and analysis of the Lowry method over the long run will indicate that it has consistently come out ahead.

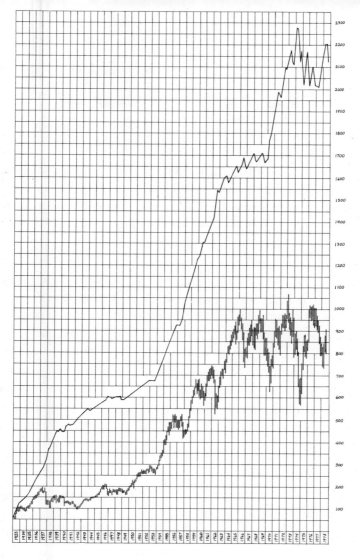

**Chart 7** The Lowry Performance chart: Lowry's buy and sell performance versus the Dow Averages for almost five decades. This is a remarkable Dowbeater forecasting record that has existed throughout war, inflation, boom, depression, bear markets, bull markets and sideways markets. (*Chart courtesy of Lowry's Reports*)

# References

BISHOP, E. L. III, and J. R. ROLLINS. "Lowry's Reports: A Denial of Market Efficiency?" *The Journal of Portfolio Management* (Fall 1977), 21–27.

DESMOND, PAUL. Interview in *The Financial Planner* (October 1977), 12–15.

LEISNER, SUSAN WAGNER. "The Lowry Fund: Florida's Unique Entry in the Mutual Fund Contest," *Florida Trend* (October 1977), 67–69.

LOWRY'S REPORTS, INC. Lowry Financial Services Corp., 350 Royal Palm Way, Palm Beach, Fla. 33480. 1970.

PETERS, JOHN. "The Lowry Legacy: What He's Left May Lead to Astonishing Stock Profits for Some," *The Florida Times-Union Jacksonville Journal* (July 24, 1977), Section H, p. 1.

# 6

# The Herzfeld Hedge: Recovering a Billion Dollars in Asset Value

## An Inductive Stock-Market Timing Approach

A major phenomenon of the market that many investors overlook is the tendency of the Dow Jones Averages to mirror the performance of the Standard & Poor's 500 Index. So closely do they correspond that it is difficult to tell which is which, when comparing them. This indicates that the performance of a portfolio of thirty stocks is almost identical over a period of time to a portfolio of five hundred stocks. In fact, once most portfolios reach a variety of more than about a dozen stocks overall, performance seems to be virtually locked into the performance of the Averages.

With this in mind, it is easy to see why it is probably better for an investor to shop for a portfolio rather than build one. Closed-end funds are ideal for this purpose because they consist of portfolios of high-quality investment grade stocks that can be purchased for $.70 or better on the dollar of asset value. To elaborate:

Unlike regular open-end mutual funds, closed-end funds issue fixed numbers of shares and do not continuously redeem their shares. Instead of buying and selling shares directly from mutual fund companies, investors in closed-end funds must buy and sell their shares through the exchanges. The only way to buy a closed-end fund is from a selling stockholder, not directly from the fund, as in open-end funds. The only way to sell a closed-end fund is to someone interested in buying the shares in the open market; they are not redeemed at their net asset value as in open-ends. In addition, since most closed-end funds are listed on an exchange, they can be traded on margin; open-end funds cannot be traded on margin.

Prices for closed-end funds are determined by the balance of supply and demand, not their net asset value. The result is that there are often times when a portfolio of blue-chip stocks that is of equal quality to the portfolio of an open-end fund can be purchased at bargain prices. These opportunities are due to short-term market factors. When these funds are being sold at steep discounts from their net asset value, they are an ideal way by which to beat the market averages.

The discount is the difference between the market price of the investment company's stock and the asset value of its underlying portfolio. Because of the widespread investor disillusionment with stocks in general, funds are now selling at a discount from net asset value. According to Thomas J. Herzfeld, the leading authority on closed-end funds,*

> There are some objective reasons why a fund should sell at a discount. For instance, a few of the funds have unrealized capital gains which, when realized and distributed, would result in a tax liability for the stockholders. It is interesting, however, that some of those funds are selling at a smaller discount than are funds with relatively small or no unrealized capital gains. Other reasons for discounts include: disappointment with performance, lack of sponsorship (most brokers recommend funds where there is higher compensation), and tax selling.

Closed-end funds do not always sell at discounts. During periods of market speculation, such as that which occurred in 1968, many were sold at net asset value and some at a small premium. Some funds are currently selling at premiums. Examples are ASA and sometimes Petroleum Corp.

Two additional factors must be considered regarding the performance of closed-end funds: first, the commission, which for a $10 stock would be about one-half point for a round trip. Second and more important is the movement of the discount. As Herzfeld points out, "Each fund tends to have its own normal discount.

*Herzfeld is an allied member of the New York Stock Exchange, Inc., a registered options principal; executive vice-president and a director of Bishop, Rosen & Co., Inc., and a member of both the New York and American Stock Exchanges. He has been a guest lecturer at the NYSE, a guest on several stock-market television shows, and is frequently quoted in leading financial publications.

Mr. Herzfeld is considered by many to be the leading expert on the subject of closed-end funds. His activities in the field include: trading, positioning and placing blocks, hedging, hedging funds against options, making markets, managing discretionary accounts, conducting and publishing research. He is the author of *Strategies for Closed-End Funds: The Herzfeld Hedge.*

"The basis for the determination of the discount is essentially to construct a moving average of the fund's discount and then adjust the figure based on eighteen variables. Some of the variables, of course, are given more weight than others.

"The key factor is to buy only when the discount is excessively large. Although "excessively large" varies from fund to fund, for aggressive accounts, "excessively large" would usually be a 5 percent deviation beyond its normal discount; for conservative accounts, this would usually mean a 10 percent deviation beyond normal.

"With the net asset value (NAV) at $10 and the discount at 30 percent (10 percent deviation), after commission of one-quarter point, the purchase price would be $7.25 ($10 minus 30 percent discount, plus one-quarter point commission). If the Dow then moved to 1100, the NAV would probably move to approximately $11. During this rise, the discount would tend to "normalize" to 20 percent, or perhaps swing to the narrow side, to 10 percent. Discounts of closed-end funds often narrow, beyond "normal," in rising markets because of investor confidence and/or enthusiasm. When the fund is sold, with the Dow then being at 1100, the net price may be 9⅝. Computed as follows: NAV $11, minus discount of 10 percent, equals $9.90, less one-quarter point commission, would be 9⅝. The profit would have been 2⅜ points or 32.8 percent during a 10 percent rise in the market.

"If the market had declined 10 percent, from 1000 to 900, the following may have occurred: With the Dow at 1000 we would have paid $7.25, as in our previous example. After the Dow declines to 900, the NAV would be approximately $8. The discount may have normalized to 20 percent. At a 20 percent discount, the price would be $7.20, minus a one-quarter point commission, netting $6.95—a net loss of $.30, or about 4 percent.

"*Caution:* what I have described in this example is what could happen, not what always *does* happen. However, a 20 to 30 percent profit objective, given a 10 percent rise in the Dow, would not be an unreasonable objective.

"For an actual example of what was just described, the reader can examine the movement of Madison Fund (MAD).

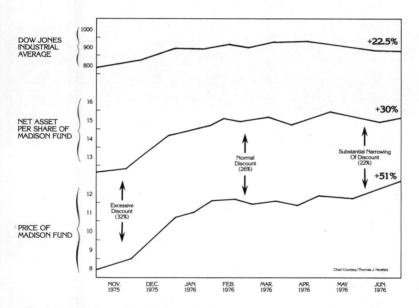

**Chart 8**    Madison Fund: In relation to its net asset value and the Dow Averages, this shows the performance possible during market upmoves. Conversely, during market declines, buying at substantial discounts below net asset value provides an important cushion from market setbacks.

"In December of 1975, MAD was selling at 8⅝ and its NAV was $12.67. It was selling at the necessary deviation from its 'normal discount,' the discount then being 31.9 percent, to be bought for aggressive accounts. The Dow then stood at 818. During the next five months, the Dow rose 22.5 percent to 1002. The NAV of MAD rose to $16.52, or a 30 percent increase. As the market climbed, the discount narrowed to about 20 percent and the price of MAD went to $13, a gain of 51 percent, while the Dow gained 22.5 percent. The above 51 percent gain does not include the $.30 in dividends paid during the period, nor does it assume any leverage (margin) which would have brought the profit to over 100 percent.

"In summary, closed-end funds offer very superior capital gains potential in the rising markets, combined with a possible cushion if the investor misjudges the market and buys into what turns out to be a declining market. A word of caution: if the "normal" discount is not judged correctly, it can work as much against the investor as for him. Also, not all funds' NAVs move exactly proportionately to the market. Therefore, it is essential for a trader to be familiar with the historical performance and current portfolios of any fund he considers trading."

A good low-risk approach for investors whose primary goal is income exists in closed-end funds that have income-oriented portfolios. These funds pay sometimes as much as 7–10 percent per year; their portfolios consist of bonds, convertible bonds, or utility stocks. Most of the time these funds also sell at discounts, just as the stock funds do. The same strategies that are outlined for stock funds also exist for income funds as a result, i.e., the savings as a result of the discounts can be used in the same way that they are used in stock funds.

The risks in this program are less than the risks for owning a portfolio of high-grade bonds because the portfolio is bought at a discount. The only time to be cautious of bond funds is naturally during periods of generally rising interest rates.

This strategy can result in profits of 20 percent per year (market profit plus dividend) instead of 8 percent. This can be done if the fund is bought and held until the discount narrows.

There is, of course, more to successful trading of closed-end funds than just being a discount follower. According to Herzfeld, the discount is the first of nearly 20 variables that must be examined. The others are:

1. Comparison of the quality and liquidity of the fund's portfolio with other closed-end funds;
2. Evaluation of the price movements of the fund in rising and declining markets;
3. Rating of the fund's performance;
4. Yield;
5. Does it have an automatic dividend reinvestment plan? Evaluation of that plan;
6. The disposition of the fund's portfolio in the current weak or strong groups;
7. Is the capital structure leveraged or not?
8. Management fee;
9. Portfolio turnover;
10. Volatility;
11. Is it a takeover candidate?
12. Is it likely to open end?
13. Reputation of the management;

14. Mutual fund redemptions;
15. Herzfeld Index changes;
16. Does it trade on the NYSE, ASE, or OTC?
17. Number of funds with similar objectives; and
18. Unrealized capital gains in portfolio.

Today there are almost 50 closed-end funds on the exchanges, as can be seen in Table 2. The largest of these funds is Tri-Continental Corporation, with assets of over $600 million.

## Table 2    Major closed-end stock and bond funds

**PUBLICLY TRADED FUNDS**

| Diversified Common Stock Funds | N.A. Value | Stk Price | % Diff |
|---|---|---|---|
| Adams Express | 14.26 | 12⅛ | −15.0 |
| Baker, Fentress & Co. | 63.37 | 41½ | −34.5 |
| General American Investors | 13.64 | 10⅛ | −25.8 |
| Lehman | 13.35 | 10 | −25.1 |
| Madison | 17.97 | 12⅜ | −31.1 |
| Niagara Share | 12.94 | 10⅞ | −15.9 |
| Overseas Securities | 4.40 | 3¼ | −26.1 |
| Tri-Continental | 22.58 | 18⅜ | −18.6 |
| US & Foreign Securities | 21.15 | 14¾ | −30.3 |
| **Specialized Equity and Convertible Funds** | | | |
| American General Convertible Securities | 23.59 | 16¼ | −31.1 |
| ASA | 22.74 | 26⅛ | +14.9 |
| Bancroft Convertible Fund | 22.57 | 16¾ | −25.8 |
| Castle Convertible Fund | 23.82 | 20⅝ | −13.4 |
| Central Securities | 7.87 | 5⅞ | −25.3 |
| Chase Convertible Fund of Boston | 11.35 | 8 | −29.5 |
| Claremont Capital | 12.47 | 8⅛ | −34.8 |
| Drexel Utility Shares | 20.39 | 17⅞ | −12.3 |

| | N.A. Value | Stk Price | % Diff |
|---|---|---|---|
| Japan Fund | 16.48 | 11⅝ | −29.5 |
| Nat'l Aviation | 30.88 | 25⅝ | −17.0 |
| New American Fund | 21.77 | 17¼ | −20.7 |
| Petroleum & Resources | 23.73 | 22⅛ | − 6.8 |
| RET Income Fund | 2.37 | 1⅞ | −20.9 |
| S-G Securities | 1.56 | 2⅛ | +36.2 |
| Source Capital | 19.20 | 16⅜ | −14.7 |
| Value Line | 3.88 | 2⅜ | −38.8 |

**BOND FUNDS***

| | N.A. Value | Stk Price | % Diff |
|---|---|---|---|
| American General Bond Fund | 22.64 | 21⅜ | − 5.7 |
| Bunker Hill Income Securities | 21.15 | 19½ | − 7.8 |
| Circle Income Shares | 14.08 | 14 | − 0.6 |
| CNA Income Shares | 12.71 | 11¼ | −11.5 |
| Current Income Shares | 12.61 | 11⅛ | −11.8 |
| Drexel Bond Debenture Trading Fund | 19.06 | 15 | −21.3 |
| Excelsior | 21.32 | 17⅞ | −16.2 |
| Fort Dearborn Income Securities | 15.03 | 13¼ | −11.8 |
| Hatteras Income Securities | 17.43 | 15½ | −11.1 |
| INA Investment Securities | 19.87 | 17⅜ | −12.6 |
| Independence Square Income Securities | 19.72 | 18⅜ | − 6.8 |
| Intercapital Income Securities | 21.67 | 20 | − 7.7 |
| John Hancock Investors | 21.59 | 19¾ | − 8.5 |
| John Hancock Income Securities | 17.05 | 16 | − 6.2 |
| MM Income Investors | 12.73 | 10¾ | −15.6 |
| Montgomery Street Income Shares | 21.73 | 19⅞ | − 8.5 |
| Mutual of Omaha Interest Shares | 15.80 | 13⅝ | −13.8 |
| Pacific American Interest Shares | 15.08 | 12⅞ | −14.6 |
| Saint Paul Securities | 12.14 | 10⅝ | −12.5 |
| State Mutual Securities | 12.54 | 10⅞ | −13.3 |
| Transamerica Income Shares | 23.21 | 20¾ | −10.6 |
| USLIFE | 11.65 | 10½ | − 9.9 |

* Unaudited net asset values of closed-end bond fund shares, reported by the companies. (As of Friday, Oct. 27, 1978.)
**Source:** *Barron's*, November 6, 1978.

Table 3 presents a breakdown of the stocks in Tri-Continental's portfolio as of December 31, 1976.

## Table 3   Portfolio of investments
December 31, 1976

**COMMON STOCKS: 90.7%**

| | Shares | Value |
|---|---|---|
| **Automotive: 2.9%** | | |
| General Motors Corporation | 250,000 | $ 19,625,000 |
| **Chemical: 11.2%** | | |
| Celanese Corporation | 175,000 | $   8,618,750 |
| Christiana Securities Company | 18,700 | 2,356,200 |
| E. I. du Pont de Nemours & Company | 140,000 | 18,917,500 |
| FMC Corporation | 150,000 | 3,675,000 |
| Grace (W. R.) & Co. | 200,000 | 5,850,000 |
| Hercules Incorporated | 150,000 | 4,200,000 |
| Monsanto Company | 160,000 | 14,100,000 |
| Rohm & Haas Company | 100,000 | 4,800,000 |
| Union Carbide Corporation | 200,000 | 12,375,000 |
| | | $ 74,892,450 |
| **Coal: 1.6%** | | |
| Mapco, Inc. | 100,000 | $   4,400,000 |
| St. Joe Minerals Corporation | 150,000 | 6,281,250 |
| | | $ 10,681,250 |
| **Consumers' Goods and Services: 11.5%** | | |
| Adolph Coors Company Class B | 75,000 | $   1,537,500 |
| Anheuser-Busch, Incorporated | 200,000 | 4,625,000 |
| Avon Products, Inc. | 300,000 | 14,850,000 |
| CBS Inc. | 100,000 | 5,937,500 |
| Coca-Cola Bottling Company of Miami, Inc. | 112,500 | 1,138,500 |
| Foremost-McKesson, Inc. | 125,000 | 1,937,500 |
| Gerber Products Company | 250,000 | 6,312,500 |
| Hospital Corporation of America | 175,000 | 4,550,000 |
| Host International, Inc. | 20,900 | 242,963 |

| | Shares | Value |
|---|---|---|
| Jos. Schlitz Brewing Company | 100,000 | 1,812,500 |
| Owens-Illinois Incorporated | 150,000 | 8,437,500 |
| PepsiCo, Inc. | 125,000 | 9,953,125 |
| Philip Morris Incorporated | 250,000 | 15,437,500 |
| | | $ 76,772,088 |

**Drug: 4.8%**

| | Shares | Value |
|---|---|---|
| American Home Products Corporation | 225,000 | $ 7,200,000 |
| Bristol-Myers Company | 120,000 | 8,205,000 |
| Pfizer, Inc. | 300,000 | 8,812,500 |
| Rorer-Amchem, Inc. | 112,900 | 2,201,550 |
| Warner-Lambert Company | 175,000 | 5,403,125 |
| | | $ 31,822,175 |

**Electrical and Electronic: 4.5%**

| | Shares | Value |
|---|---|---|
| Emerson Electric Co. | 100,000 | 3,450,000 |
| Fairchild Camera & Instrument Corporation | 75,000 | 3,065,625 |
| Honeywell, Inc. | 170,000 | 8,245,000 |
| International Telephone & Telegraph Corporation | 300,000 | 10,162,500 |
| Square D Company | 197,100 | 5,494,163 |
| | | $ 30,417,288 |

**Finance and Insurance: 6.8%**

| | Shares | Value |
|---|---|---|
| American Re-Insurance Company | 296,800 | $ 6,715,100 |
| Chubb Corporation | 60,000 | 2,415,000 |
| Citicorp | 62,500 | 2,046,875 |
| Colonial Penn Group | 50,000 | 1,450,000 |
| Continental Illinois Corporation | 119,300 | 6,919,400 |
| Crocker National Corporation | 100,000 | 2,800,000 |
| Gulf Life Holding Company | 525,000 | 5,906,250 |
| Heller (Walter E.) International Corporation | 150,000 | 3,375,000 |
| Transamerica Corporation | 150,000 | 2,137,500 |
| Travelers Corporation | 160,000 | 5,880,000 |
| Western Bancorporation | 200,000 | 6,050,000 |
| | | $ 45,695,125 |

| | Shares | Value |
|---|---|---|
| **Household Equipment: 1.0%** | | |
| Maytag Company | 191,300 | $ 6,791,150 |
| | | |
| **Metals: 1.8%** | | |
| Inland Steel Company | 100,000 | 5,087,500 |
| Kaiser Steel Corporation | 80,000 | 2,620,000 |
| United States Steel Corporation | 90,000 | 4,477,500 |
| | | $ 12,185,000 |
| **Miscellaneous: 3.1%** | | |
| Allis-Chalmers Corp. | 150,000 | $ 3,881,250 |
| Avery International Corporation | 200,000 | 4,350,000 |
| Baker Industries, Inc. | 170,000 | 1,827,500 |
| Engelhard Minerals & Chemical Corporation | 150,000 | 5,025,000 |
| Minnesota Mining & Manufacturing Company | 100,000 | 5,662,500 |
| | | $ 20,746,250 |
| **Office Equipment and Supplies: 6.9%** | | |
| Burroughs Corporation | 60,000 | $ 5,497,500 |
| International Business Machines Corporation | 140,000 | 39,095,000 |
| Wallace Business Forms, Inc. | 67,000 | 1,415,375 |
| | | $ 46,007,875 |
| **Oil: 13.9%** | | |
| Continental Oil Company | 250,000 | $ 9,375,000 |
| Exxon Corporation | 300,000 | 16,087,500 |
| Mobil Corporation | 125,000 | 8,125,000 |
| Phillips Petroleum Company | 160,000 | 10,580,000 |
| Standard Oil Company of California | 500,000 | 20,500,000 |
| Standard Oil Company of Indiana | 200,000 | 11,925,000 |
| Union Oil Company of California | 275,000 | 16,293,750 |
| | | $ 92,886,250 |

| Paper: 5.7% | Shares | Value |
|---|---|---|
| Boise Cascade Corporation | 200,000 | $ 6,725,000 |
| Crown Zellerbach Corporation | 130,000 | 5,850,000 |
| Great Northern Nekoosa Corporation | 253,000 | 8,285,750 |
| Hoerner Waldorf Corporation | 75,000 | 1,762,500 |
| Kimberly-Clark Corporation | 125,000 | 5,500,000 |
| Union Camp Corporation | 150,000 | 9,993,750 |
| | | $ 38,117,000 |

| | Shares or Principal Amount | Value |
|---|---|---|
| **Public Utility: 3.7%** | | |
| Arizona Public Service Company | 200,000 | $ 3,925,000 |
| Cleveland Electric Illuminating Company | 100,000 | 3,462,500 |
| General Telephone & Electronics Corporation | 200,000 | 6,375,000 |
| Mountain Fuel Supply Company | 100,000 | 4,450,000 |
| Northern States Power Company | 50,000 | 1,475,000 |
| Pioneer Corporation | 150,000 | 5,437,500 |
| | | $ 25,125,000 |
| **Retail Trade: 5.9%** | | |
| Albertson's, Inc. | 125,000 | $ 2,890,625 |
| Allied Stores Corporation | 100,000 | 4,600,000 |
| Federated Department Stores, Inc. | 127,500 | 6,247,500 |
| House of Fabrics, Inc. | 225,000 | 1,996,875 |
| Kresge (S. S.) Company | 200,000 | 8,150,000 |
| Meyer (Fred), Inc. Class A | 85,300 | 1,929,913 |
| Safeway Stores, Inc. | 210,000 | 10,526,250 |
| Sears, Roebuck & Co. | 50,000 | 3,450,000 |
| | | $ 39,791,163 |

| | Shares or Principal Amount | Value |
|---|---|---|
| **Transportation and Equipment: 2.7%** | | |
| ACF Industries, Incorporated | 75,000 | $  2,606,250 |
| Consolidated Freightways, Inc. | 245,000 | 6,492,500 |
| Yellow Freight Systems, Inc. Class A | 200,000 | 8,625,000 |
| | | $ 17,723,750 |
| **Special Holdings: 2.4%** | | |
| American Bankers Insurance Co. of Florida | 82,200 | 452,100 |
| Burndy Corporation | 40,000 | 1,180,000 |
| Chemed Corporation | 50,000 | 1,275,000 |
| Commercial Alliance Corporation | 50,000 | 525,000 |
| Development Corporation of America | 22,000 | 132,000 |
| EG&G, Inc. | 75,000 | 1,275,000 |
| Overseas Shipholding Group, Inc. | 55,000 | 1,340,625 |
| Payless Cashways, Inc. | 30,000 | 926,250 |
| Pittway Corporation | 22,500 | 849,375 |
| Preferred Risk Life Insurance Company | 55,000 | 495,000 |
| Progressive Corporation (Ohio) | 75,000 | 796,875 |
| Russell Stover Candies, Inc. | 65,000 | 1,056,250 |
| Santa Fe International Corporation | 30,000 | 1,353,750 |
| Skaggs Companies, Inc. | 60,800 | 1,383,200 |
| Smith's Transfer Corporation | 40,000 | 715,000 |
| United Services Life Insurance Company | 80,900 | 819,113 |
| Watkins-Johnson Company | 50,000 | 1,193,750 |
| | | $ 15,768,288 |
| **Other: .3%** | | $  1,962,752 |
| Total Common Stocks (cost $425,348,940) | | $607,009,854 |
| **CONVERTIBLE SECURITIES: 2.3%** | | |
| Atlantic Richfield Co. $2.80 Pfd. | 80,000 | $  5,770,000 |
| Champion International Corp. $1.20 Pfd. | 60,000 | 1,650,000 |

| | Shares or Principal Amount | Value |
|---|---|---|
| Mesa Petroleum Co. $1.60 Pfd. | 100,000 | 3,637,500 |
| Sperry Rand Deb. 6%, 2000 | $4,000,000 | 4,520,000 |
| Total Convertible Securities (cost $14,825,595) | | $ 15,577,500 |

| | Principal Amount | Value |
|---|---|---|
| **BONDS: .4%** | | |
| Marcor Installment Sub. Deb. 6½%, 1988 | $ 115,000 | $ 101,200 |
| Monitor Investing Secured Notes 5¼%, 1986 | 147,772 | 120,246* |
| Tenneco Deb. 7%, 1993 | 2,965,000 | 2,642,556 |
| Total Bonds (cost $3,044,058) | | $ 2,864,002 |
| Short Term Holdings: 9.2% | | $ 61,867,519 |
| Other Assets Less Liabilities: (2.6%) | | $ (17,266,526) |
| Net Investment Assets: 100.0% | | $670,052,349 |

There is a total of over a billion dollars of assets existing between the present prices of all the closed-end funds and their net asset value. Obviously, then, closed-end funds have tremendous advantages both for the long-term investor and for trading purposes.

*Business Week Letter*, in an interview with Herzfeld, summarizes the advantages of trading closed-end funds as follows:

1. Closed-end funds also can offer more protection than an individual stock in a down market. If you buy a fund which is selling at an excessively sharp discount from net asset value, a decline in the stock market will prob-

ably have little effect on the market price of the fund. That's because the fund is selling at a discount from the assets in its portfolio—and hence the assets have to fall dramatically to affect the market price of the fund.

2. Even more important is the leverage which closed-end stock funds give investors. Investors who buy wisely could outperform the market averages by a ratio of at least 2–3 times. As the stock market rallies, not only will the assets in the portfolio move, but the discount from net asset value will probably shrink. That's because investors tend to get more enthusiastic about funds during a rally—and hence bid up their prices.

3. Even if the assets in the fund's portfolio don't increase during the rally, investors can make a sizeable profit. Take a fund which has a net asset value of $10 a share, but is selling for $7—an excessively large 30% discount from net asset value. If that discount shrinks to only 10% (not an unreasonable expectation during a rally) the fund's shares would jump to $9, giving you a 30% return on investment.*

*Kiril Sokoloff. "The Open End in Closed-End Stock Funds," *The Business Week Letter*, (29 November 1976).

# PART THREE
# DOWBEATER
# INVESTMENTS

# 7

# The Specific Selection
# of Dowbeater Stocks

Investment philosophy, with respect to common stocks, has changed notably in the twentieth century. In the early 1920s few utility stocks outside of AT&T and Consolidated Edison were included among the elite blue chips. The favorite shares then were U.S. Steel, Pullman Company, New York Central, Pennsylvania Railroad, Union Pacific, American Tobacco, Allied Chemical, and General Motors. The stress was on seasoned shares of great companies and dividend dependability. The expression "growth stock" was not yet in the financial vocabulary.

By the end of the 1920s, however, market preferences had changed. Not just the rich, the prudent, and the thrifty were stock buyers, but a whole new postwar generation of speculators entered "the market." They cared little about dividend income; they wanted to run a modest stake into a killing by active speculation in what proved, from 1926 to 1929, to be a roaring bull market. Many lacked the resources, the knowledge, or the experience to trade or invest in stocks intelligently; but they were caught up in the market mania. And it took so little money to get started! In that era you could buy $1000 worth of stocks with only a 10 percent margin ($100).

Stocks seemed to go up every day. The active favorites on the Big Board were Radio Corp. (the technology company of the era, comparable with Zenith, TRW, or Perkin-Elmer today), Montgomery Ward, Technicolor (which went over $100 in 1929 and sold at $1 in 1933); and over-the-counter bank and insurance shares. National City Bank reached $540 in 1929. The "new game in town" was in utility holding companies. Middle West Utilities, Cities Service, North American Company, Utilities Power & Light, Associated Gas & Electric all zoomed to giddy heights on highly pyramided capitalizations.

The crazy game ended in 1932 with the DJI at 42, down from 340 in 1929. Hundreds of thousands of individuals were wiped out when stock prices plummeted. They couldn't answer the "margin calls" for more money or collateral and were swiftly sold out, with each distressing day of liquidating sending the market lower. There was a short-lived bounce back in 1930, but then the Depression set in with a vengeance, bottoming out in 1932. It was not until twenty years later that the memory of this debacle was sufficiently erased, and conditions sufficiently improved, to once again attract middle-class America back into the stock market.

In the era after World War II, confidence and enthusiasm slowly rekindled. Major technological advances brought forth fabulous new industries: television, computers, data processing, wonder drugs, air conditioning, copying machines, jet planes, air transport companies, atomic power, etc. A whole new industrial world was born. Stock investing in the 1950s was not primarily for income, but for long-term gain via "growth stocks" which retained and plowed back earnings rather than distributing cash dividends. Investors in growth stocks were generously rewarded by frequent extra dividends in stock and split-ups; and by occasional dramatic rises in share prices. The market darlings of the 1950s included Columbia Broadcasting, Trans World Air, Xerox, IBM, Admiral, Zenith, Merck, Pfizer, Denison Mines (uranium), Boeing, Douglas Aircraft, G.D. Searle, 3M; and life insurance stocks: Franklin, National Life & Accident, Republic National, etc.

Later favorites from the 1960s to date would include convenience foods: Kentucky Fried Chicken, McDonald's, Howard Johnson; motel chains: Marriott, Ramada, Hilton, Sheraton, Holiday Inns; and zooming and plunging equities like Winnebago (motor homes), Levitz (furniture), and Hy-Gain (CB radios). Perkin-Elmer, bank holding companies: Frank B. Hall, Marsh & McLennan (insurance brokerage), and (since 1972) gold stocks were all winners.

The market panorama is ever-changing, with the favorite of one decade often the "dog" of the next. Some of these swings and preferences are capricious; others are dictated by changed economic conditions and visible declines in the profitability of particular industries. Caprice (and high gasoline prices) battered motor home companies in the 1970s; low cost and hungry copper-producing countries—Peru, Chile, and Zaire—knocked down copper prices to the anguish of Kennecott, Asarco, Texgulf, Hecla, etc.; and overbuilding as well as overmortgaging made real-estate investment trusts a disaster area. Regardless of cause of the component elements, the stock market was not "bouncy" in the 1970s.

The foregoing brief reviews of varying market enthusiasms and disenchantments bring us up, at rather high velocity, to 1978, and prompts a couple of basic questions. Is the stock market a valid sector for prudent investment during 1979-80? Is it possible to select issues whose total returns (dividends plus increases in market value) can: (1) at least equal the 9 percent total annual return achieved on representative blue-chip stocks 1926–76; and (2) possibly expand in value at a faster rate than current inflation? (We have, of course, assumed as a basic premise that Dowbeater stock selections should consistently outperform the DJI.)

Our answer to these questions is: Yes. But winning procedures in portfolio management today may well diverge from the traditions of the past. The fashionable stocks of bygone years may no longer prove desirable or rewarding. A new approach, consideration of newer industries, and a more incisive analysis of corporate managements may now be required.

Many corporations that earned well in the past now have "tired" managements. Further, diversification, which used to be so revered in security accounts, is less valued today. What counts is not how many issues you hold but how dynamic they are! For any portfolio up to $250,000 ten issues, if they are well screened, should prove adequate. Diversification is not a sacred ritual. It was merely designed to assure: (1) that a single unfortunate investment would not demolish one's net worth, and (2) some breadth of representation in sound companies in different economic sectors, so that if stocks in one industry were in a profit slowdown, other issues owned might offset declines in value or dividends by their superior performances.

We hold to no fixed points such as that some percentage of a portfolio should be in utilities, so much in industrials, so much in insurance or banking, so much in bonds, etc. We definitely take the view that the quality of the company and its potentials for rising profits and dividends are more important than general selection of securities by the industries they are in. Obviously, however, we would favor companies in promising rather than declining economic sectors.

With this background reference, we are now ready to set down some useful criteria for Dowbeater stocks, and to follow with a screened list of diversified securities meeting, in most particulars, these time-tested specifications.

A Dowbeater stock should be: (1) in a significant company (but not necessarily the leader in its industry) and in a visible or anticipated uptrend (this includes turn-around situations); (2) increasing its revenues at the rate of at least 12 percent annually; and its net profits at a rate of 12 percent or higher; (3) showing a return of 15 percent or more on stockholders' equity (book value); (4) capitalized no higher than 25 percent in long-term debt, with 75 percent equity; (5) established for at least five years; (6) grossing at least $5 million annually; (7) displaying energetic, innovative, and cost-conscious management; (8) substantially stock owned by officers and directors (20 percent or more) to properly motivate management and to fend off unwanted takeover bids; (9) owned by at least 1000 stockholders to assure reasonable marketability (the number of stockholders should be on the increase); (10) able to show a record or capability of rising dividend payments in cash, stock, or both; (11) known for the quality of its products or services, and absence of hazard or risk to users (product liability); (12) excellent in research and development of new or improved products or services; (13) free from foreign competition; (14) low cost in labor (low percentage labor to gross revenues and, preferably, nonunion to assure quality controls and insure against costly strikes that delay deliveries to customers); (15) market-sponsored by original underwriter, responsible broker/dealers, or effective floor broker (if issue is listed), any of whom may supply current information about the company to investors and to the financial community; and (16) in the case of natural resources companies, able to show ample proven reserves of petroleum, minerals, or timber.

Further, to be an attractive purchase, the issue under consideration should be available at or below eight times earnings, and below its book value.

Common stocks that qualify in most of these respects should prove acceptable purchases, under average market conditions.

Timing of the actual purchase should be checked by references to the altitude of DJI, possibly a Dow Theory chart, or a bar chart showing the current technical position of the stock, its indicated trendline, and trading volume. If an issue closes higher for several days in a row on large and rising volume, it is thought to be under accumulation. On the contrary, if it sells at lower closing prices for several days running, the issue may be under liquidation, and purchase, however fundamentally indicated, may be prudently deferred.

These criteria are by no means absolute and unwavering. The final characteristics of winning stocks are market recognition and sponsorship. These elements are generated not only by traders, customers' brokers, and analysts, but from reports and write-ups by brokerage houses and investment advisory services; and from items, comment, or even feature articles in the *Wall Street Journal, Barron's, Forbes, Fortune,* the *Market Chronicle,* the *Financial World,* and the financial pages of metropolitan dailies.

Once a stock gets popular (by recognition and sponsorship) it may increase its times/earnings multiple at a notably faster rate than gains in its net profits and become a trading favorite. Over the long run, stock prices are the slaves of earning power. Don't expect a stock to move up with animation unless its earnings also are moving up. Past earnings and earlier "highs"' for the stock are not necessarily reliable guides as to future performance.

## Dowbeater Selections

In the pages immediately following, we outline several stock issues that could prove rewarding within the next two years. We introduce these without a whisper of recommendation or endorsement, but rather as examples of issues likely to attract speculators and to provide above-average total returns over a reasonable period.

Our first selection is Dome Petroleum Ltd. We regard it as among the elite North American resource stocks, a major Canadian oil and gas producer and pipeline operator with a significant stage in Beaufort Sea drilling exploration.

Dome has working interests in 43,143,000 gross (22,529,000 net) acres of oil and gas rights and 26,570,000 gross royalty acres. Recoverable reserves totaled 307.6 million (gross) barrels of crude oil, natural gas liquids, and oil equivalents (excluding Arctic islands).

Dome also operates, and owns, 50 percent of Natural Gas Liquids System, with extraction and processing plants, gas pipelines, and underground storage tanks. Further, it has a $150 million investment commitment in the construction of a huge petrochemical facility in Alberta (in association with Dow Chemical and Alberta Gas Trunk Line) to cost $1.5 billion. Of major immediate interest are Dome's extensive holdings in the Elmwood and West Pembina areas of Alberta, where 1977–78 exploration indicated important gas strikes.

Dome Petroleum owns a 29.5 percent interest in Dome Mines, which in turn controls Campbell Red Lake, the richest gold mine in Canada, as well as the Dome and Sigma gold mines; and has a 14 percent interest in Canada Tungsten, Ltd.

Gross and net revenues are both in a strong uptrend; there are 12,152,346 common shares of DMP (trading symbol) listed on the Toronto, Montreal, and American Stock Exchanges, preceded by $436,519,000 in long-term debt. No cash dividends have been paid, but there was a 200 percent stock dividend in 1971. We would anticipate another sizable stock dividend and then possibly cash dividends (to make the issue acceptable for pension funds).

Within the next two years we expect a significant advance in the market price of DMP. It is an equity of unusual merit, not yet attracting the following to which it is entitled. As of November 3, 1978, Dome sold for 64⅛.

## Koger Properties, Inc.

Metropolitan real estate has a great future, especially under inflationary conditions. One of the best-managed public companies in this industry is Koger Properties, Inc. It owns and operates metropolitan office buildings. Shares in this company offer the prospect of rising revenues and earnings, substantial and rising cash flow, tax-free dividends (a return of capital), and enhancing asset value per share.

Koger, headquartered in Jacksonville, Florida, specializes in the construction and operation of modern office-building centers in rapidly growing cities in the South and Southwest.

The company's policy is to sell off, when desirable, substantial interests in its properties, generating capital gains and rising cash flow leading to higher dividends. Koger also derives fees from continued management of properties sold; and gains from selling off portions of raw land owned. Properties appear to be undervalued at $149.8 million, against estimated replacement cost of about $200 million. Cash flow is growing at the rate of about 15 percent a year. Gross rentals were $21,114,000 in fiscal 1977 (year ends 3/31), up from $8,837,000 in 1973.

There are 4,514,000 shares of common outstanding, leveraged by long-term debt of $132 million.

Stock trades in OTC market under symbol KOGR, on November 3, 1978, at 13¾.

## Datapoint Corporation

When people talk about computers generally, they refer to IBM, Sperry Rand, Burroughs, Honeywell, Digital Equipment. There are, however, a number of other companies in this sophisticated field that have staked out their own sectors of the market and moved rapidly forward by technological excellence and marketing competence. Among such lesser-known companies is Datapoint Corporation, a thriving enterprise headquartered in San Antonio, Texas, where its total facilities occupy approximately 468,000 feet of space. A division, Western Development Center in Berkeley, California, features software. A subsidiary, Amcomp Inc. (formerly called Data Disc, Inc.), acquired 1/17/77, is a quality producer of disc and tape drives for sale to original equipment makers. There are also manufacturing facilities in Sunnyvale, California, a factory in Singapore, and forty US marketing offices.

Datapoint now offers seven basic general purpose business processors, varying in speed, memory, and capability. Larger units include the 2200, the 5500, and the 6000, a processor designed for sophisticated use and tied into twenty-four terminals.

Recently Datapoint introduced a new major system-oriented, primarily software-based product. This is a package of system programs that utilizes a microprocessor controlled coaxial cable as the device to tie individual operations of many intelligent terminals and processors. What all this fancy equipment does is to localize computer operations, rather than have them all clustered in one central computer center. It preserves the capability of individual business departments to control their own data-processing needs. Datapoint markets its products in the United States through its own direct sales force and supportive systems engineers. Products are marketed to end users in fifty countries.

Datapoint, which grosses over $100 million annually, is not as well known as it should be. It may prove a market virtuoso among the current crop of glamour stocks. It is already the leader in dispersed data processing and in communications management.

Datapoint common, 3,330,000 shares outstanding, trades on NYSE under symbol DPT, November 3, 1978, 56½.

## National Environmental Controls Inc.

This is an early phase company in the collection and disposal of waste materials and owns the patented Chemfix process that converts urban and industrial wastes into environmentally acceptable products.

Headquartered in Metaire, Louisiana, National Environmental Controls has expanded its original business of handling solid waste disposal in communities in the vicinity of New Orleans and Birmingham. Wastes gathered are transported to sanitary landfills and the service is being expanded to other communities.

The particular "romance" in the company, however, is the acquisition (7/21/77) of the assets of Chemfix Stockholders' Trust of Pittsburgh. The purchase agreement includes world rights and patents for the process of controlling most organic and inorganic hazardous wastes, which currently cause land and/or water pollution. According to Daniel N. Silverman, Jr., president of National, "the hazardous waste field is a multi-billion dollar market and we believe the acquisition of Chemfix puts National into a position of industrial leadership."

Another interesting corporate facet is National's contract to supply garbage to a new $75 million plant at Taft, Louisiana, to be built by Hooker Division of Occidental Petroleum, to process and burn garbage at its nearby chemical plant. National will not only supply the raw material but participate as a partner in the venture.

There are 2,787,116 shares of NECT (trading symbol on OTC market) quoted around 2½. A long-shot speculation for those with sporting blood, and perhaps a winner.

## Kennametal Inc.

This leading manufacturer of tungsten products earns about 16 percent on stockholders' equity and has increased its dividends regularly for many years. It is a unique industrial equity with visible gainful potentials.

Kennametal does not mine this amazingly hard and heat-resistant metal, tungsten. It is, however, a recognized leader in the manufacture of tungsten products, including: (1) drills, bits, cutters, toolholders, rotating tools used in the metalworking industry; (2) mining and construction tools, including tungsten carbide-tipped bits demanded in the coal and mining industry, and snowplow and grader blades; (3) metallurgical powders; (4) defense items such as armor-defeating ammunition for the US government. Tungsten has been described as "the cutting edge of the world."

Kennametal serves more than 30,000 customers and provides over 10,000 stock items and many specialty products. It is a research-oriented company, concentrating on the metallurgy of tungsten and developing a continuous flow of new products to meet a broad spectrum of human needs.

While some of the markets served, particularly the metal-working industry, are cyclical in nature, Kennametal has so diversified its operations as to provide consistent year-to-year growth. Its earnings have increased at a rate of 12 percent compounded for the past ten years. With coal mining and oil drilling in strong uptrends, the company should be able to maintain this growth rate.

There are 5,928,000 shares of KDP (NYSE trading symbol) outstanding, preceded by only $12.6 million in long-term debt. The dividend of $1.08 could easily be increased. Sales for (fiscal) 1977 were $166.4 million (and heading for $200 million in 1978) and book value at the year end was $19.30 per share. Kennametal common at 32 merits investor attention because of the essentiality of company products and the enhancement of product line, profits, and dividends.

## Rollins Burdick Hunter Co.

This is one among the substantial group of companies rapidly gaining in business volume and stature in the insurance brokerage industry. Leaders include Marsh & McLennan, Alexander & Alexander, and Frank B. Hall. All these companies have done well but currently growing at a faster rate is our selection, Rollins Burdick Hunter Co., headquartered in Chicago.

RBHC (OTC trading symbol for the common stock) conducts an expanding and international insurance agency business, primarily in the placing property and casualty insurance with underwriters on behalf of large corporate clients; and placing, to a lesser degree, marine, life, accident, and health insurance. The insurance brokerage business is a strong trend toward consolidation. Independent local or regional agencies find they can control large corporate accounts better by joining forces with nationwide firms. That way they offer broader and more complete service to clients, and develop more "clout" with insuring institutions because of the volume of premium business they can deliver.

Rollins Burdick has been an aggressive and successful

consolidator, having acquired thirteen brokerage firms since it went public in 1970. By these strategic additions, RBHC has rounded out a full service organization; and the company may be expected by future expansion to increase its market penetration further. There are 3,735,646 common shares trading OTC at 21¼ November 3, 1978. A lively stock with a bright future.

## DeBeers Consolidated Mines Ltd.

DeBeers Consolidated Mines Ltd. is the General Motors of the diamond industry, and a remarkably well-managed, high-profit organization. Its principal drawback in the investment community is that it is domiciled in South Africa. DeBeers specializes in gemstone diamonds which account for only 20 percent of annual world production of 50 million carats, but 80 percent of the value of mine output. DeBeers accounts for approximately 25 percent of world diamond production and 45 percent of gemstones. Through its Central Selling Organization, DeBeers distributes over 80 percent of the world's rough diamond production (including sales for Russia, outside that nation). It marketed over $2½ billion in 1978!

Diamonds have been in strong demand as choice personal holdings, especially in time of inflation; and the market comfortably absorbed a 5 percent price increase in March 1977, and a further 17 percent increase in uncut gem diamonds in December 1977, and further increases in 1978.

While diamonds are the major source of earning power, the company develops a rich annual cash flow providing funds for substantial investments in other fields; manufacturing, real estate, gold, platinum, copper, and coal mining.

Investments outside the diamond industry are valued at above $750 million; and generated over $55 million in annual income.

DeBeers has 359.8 million shares outstanding, trading in the U.S. in ADR's, quoted November 3, 1978 at 5.

In view of the remarkable earning power of DeBeers, its generous dividend payments, its low P/E multiple (around three times), and the increased worldwide diversification of its earning assets, DeBeers has the attributes of a gainful long-term investment.

## Credithrift Financial, Inc.

Credithrift Financial, Inc., headquartered in Evansville, Indiana, is a holding company with subsidiaries principally engaged in consumer finance and insurance.

The company has 535 consumer loan and finance offices in twenty-six states. These offices make direct installment loans to families and individuals, and finance purchases by buying installment sales contracts from dealers of durable goods.

A substantial insurance business is done through wholly owned Yosemite Insurance Co. and its subsidiary, Great Falls Insurance Co. The Yosemite group, based in San Francisco, writes multiple-line property and casualty insurance specializing in credit-oriented coverages.

CRD, listed on NYSE November 3, 1978 7⅝ appears as an aggressive financial institution operating in the same loan market in which Household Finance has been a consistent winner.

## Hanover Insurance Company

During 1974 and 1975, casualty insurance stocks were in the doldrums, as premium income failed to keep pace with losses experienced and claim settlements in an inflationary economy. Beginning in mid-1976, however, the outlook of the industry improved as rate increases were widely instituted, risks were more intensively screened, and portfolio incomes expanded. Further, the average return on insurance company investments had been in a rising trend for a decade.

Among companies in line to benefit from this improved business climate is Hanover Insurance Co., an elite veteran in the industry. Hanover has been in business for 126 years and has paid dividends without interruption since 1853! The company ranks among the oldest property/casualty insurers in America and markets its product through some 2800 independent agents in the United States and Canada.

Since 1968, State Mutual Life Insurance Co., headquartered in Worcester, Massachusetts, has owned 48 percent of the 3,236,000 shares of Hanover outstanding. State Mutual is the twentieth largest life insurance company in America. State Mutual, Hanover Insurance, plus a mutual fund company, Colonial Management, operate under a common banner, "The America Group."

Hanover, selling at 23½ November 3, 1978 in the OTC market, may be a notable performer with earnings above $9 a share, and capability of substantial dividend increase from present rate, $.28, and selling below book value (about $29 a share).

## Buckeye Federal Savings and Loan Association

The savings and loan industry in the United States is the major financial vehicle for mortgage finance of individual homes. These S & Ls are of four sorts: those under federal or state charter; those that are mutual (depositor-owned), and those owned by public shareholders. In any event, the industry has grown rapidly and investors in public companies have done well.

Of particular interest to investors, however, is a new trend—the conversion of mutual S & Ls into stock companies. Many mutuals have found their capacity to lend money, and to grow, has been restricted by insufficient capital. They were limited to capital and surplus funds originally supplied, augmented by additions to surplus from earnings retained year by year. This rate of capital growth has proved inadequate for many progressive S & Ls.

A good example of a company going public in this industry is Buckeye Federal Savings and Loan Association of Columbus, Ohio. To generate more capital and thus take better advantage of its lending opportunities, Buckeye, after decades as a mutual institution (since 1895), became in 1976 a federally chartered public company. After a 25 percent stock dividend in May 1978, Buckeye has outstanding 1,530,037 capital shares trading in the OTC market under symbol BFSA at 11¾ on November 3, 1978. With assets in excess of $800 million Buckeye now ranks among the one hundred largest S & Ls in the U.S.

Buckeye is the leading real estate mortgage lender in mid-Ohio, serving Columbus (Franklin County) and six surrounding counties. Buckeye is a member of the Federal Home Banking System, and conducts its business through eighteen offices and thirty-four remote service offices (mostly in supermarkets in the area). Buckeye makes all the standard loans on residential property plus VA, FHA, construction, and development loans.

We think Buckeye is ably managed and expansion-oriented. Its common stock should continue to outpace the Dow average.

## Schlumberger Ltd.

Schlumberger is an elite company and a dominant force in the oil industry. It features a computerized "logging" process that evaluates oil wells and enables drillers to determine whether or not a new well is properly productive. In providing this logging service, Schlumberger enjoys about 70 percent of the world market.

The company is really big, grossing $2.2 billion in 1977, which it converted into $401 million of net profits. Its growth rate is quite remarkable—35 percent annually for the past six years; and fourteen years during which, in each quarter, net profits exceeded the preceding quarter. With oil production expanding all over the world, SLB (NYSE symbol for the common stock) should continue its progress.

Two new processes should stimulate customer growth: a (long-researched) generation of tools to define the production potential of a well, marketed by SLB's wireline division; and "measurement-while-drilling" (MWB), a remarkable new instrument giving fifteen assorted readings from the bottom of the hole and permitting fast, safer, more efficient drilling.

This opens up a whole new, high-profit field for the company —analyzing rock formations and supplementing existing logging techniques.

When large capital outlays are made to drill oil wells, it is important that the money not be wasted. For relatively low cost (about 3½ percent of total drilling outlay) SLB's devices can be applied to maximize the profitability of the drilling effort.

Here's a stock of rare quality, paying a $1.40 dividend (likely to be increased). Further, the stock could very well be split so that it would trade in a more popular price range. Current price, Nov. 3, 1978, is $88. (On the same date, the DJIA stood at 823.)

We have outlined above a group of companies that fit in generally quite well with the criteria we drew up earlier in this chapter. It is by no means a complete list. Other companies favored on our shopping list would include Perkin-Elmer, a steadily expanding scientific company; Overseas Shipholding Corp., perhaps the best-managed American company in ocean transportation; Ohio Casualty, a topflight insurance company; American Income Life, one of the fastest-growing life insurance companies; Frank B. Hall, a virtuoso in insurance brokerage; Ranier National Bank and Idaho First National Bank, splendidly managed commercial banks; Pentair, outstanding producer of coated papers for the publishing industry; Total Petroleum, a dynamic US/Canadian hydrocarbon producer; National Mine Safety, a beneficiary of the expanding coal industry; Denison Mines, the leading North American uranium producer; ERGO, a South African company with a sophisticated low-cost process for gleaning gold and uranium from millions of tons of waste mining slimes; Kenton Co., a highly leveraged holding company (OTC); Lubrizol, the elite company in petroleum additives; Canada Tungsten, the leading independent tungsten producer in North America; Campbell Red Lake, the best Canadian gold mine; Bally Mfg., the leader in pinball and slot machines for gambling casinos; and Rapid-American Corp.

This chapter is designed to aid you specifically in the selection of winning stocks (Dowbeaters), using benchmarks that have served well in the past. *We expect these stocks to continue to outperform the Dow during its forthcoming explosive moves, and therefore these stocks will continue to represent outstanding leadership in the coming Grand Supercycle.* The issues mentioned are believed to have above-average merit, but there are hundreds of other promising stocks among the 40,000 issues traded each week; so keep your eyes open and look for unheralded companies.

Finally, these are the four essential guidelines for investing in Dowbeater selections: select each security carefully by getting complete current information about it; time your purchases well; be a patient investor, not a frantic trader; and have both an objective and a target for each purchase. Plan to sell a stock when its earning curve flattens out, when you need the money, when you are satisfied with the gain you've made, when the growth prospects of an industry have peaked; and sell "when the clamor of the bulls is loudest." In highly speculative plays, try "operation bait back"—when a stock gains over 200 percent, automsticaly sell half and keep the other half.

# B

# Bank Stocks as Dowbeaters

Curiously, most books on common stock investments pay little attention to bank shares, yet they rank among the oldest and most desirable of equities both for dividend income and dependable growth. Well-chosen bank shares, particularly those located in sections of the country displaying rapid economic growth, are gainful securities capable of outpacing the DJI year after year.

There is something special about bank stocks. In most of the cities in the United States, you will find that leading citizens and the wealthier members of the community own bank stocks. Many individuals own sizable blocks of bank shares, and it is customary to find "fat cats" placed on the board of directors of their local banks as a mark of status and stature. Indeed, as press speculations about Bert Lance in 1977 intimated, sometimes being a bank director may give you special access to sizable lines of credit!

Another clue to the desirability of bank shares is found in the investments of our congressmen. In metropolitan newspaper articles during May of 1978, some description was given of the investment holdings of our congressional representatives. Of the four hundred representatives included in the reports, almost all owned real estate; quite a few had no common stocks, but of those who did, the favorite kind was bank stocks. Good bank stocks are elite investments and some are attractive vehicles for capital gains.

Commercial banks are among the oldest of American corporations. The first in business was The Bank of New York, founded in 1778; many other banks have been in continuous operation for more than a century. There are now approximately 14,800 commercial banks in America, including state and national banks. National banks must be stockholders in the Federal Reserve Bank, and keep specified minimum deposits at the Federal Reserve Bank in their district. National banks also have the privilege of borrowing money from "the Fed" and paying the prevailing "rediscount rate," which is regularly referred to in the financial press as one of the more important economic barometers.

Banks, particularly "state" banks, blossomed like clover in the nineteenth century. They could be opened then with relatively small amounts of capital, and they received deposits, provided checking, made loans, and even issued their own paper money. In times of economic stress, however, the "paper" dollars of small local banks were accepted only at a discount; and in the recurrent depressions of the 1800s bank failures were commonplace.

The erratic and mostly unregulated banking system of the nineteenth century led to the creation of the Federal Reserve System, in 1913, designed to provide a disciplined surveillance of the operations of member banks; a source of reserve credit; and a structure by which to prevent bank failures by periodical auditing and financial support in the event of a "run." The Fed, however, couldn't stem the tide of gross overlending during the 1920s, particularly on marketable securities; and thousands of banks failed during the Great Depression.

These failures were bitter medicine to thousands of stockholders. In that period, most bank stocks were "assessable"—that is, the registered owner could be called upon to put up the par amount of his shares in event of the bank's default on its obligations. Thus, a poor soul who owned shares in his local bank (usually of $100 par value) found that when the bank failed, his shares had no market value, and in addition he was obliged under the law to deliver $100 to the bank for each share in his name! Many individuals went bankrupt as a result of this requirement.

Since the dismal thirties, however, there have been a number of legislative and regulatory changes designed to protect both depositors and shareowners. Bank stocks no longer have the double liability. Bank deposit accounts are guaranteed up to $40,000 by Federal Deposit Insurance Corp. Banks are under the regulation variously by state banking authorities, the Comptroller of the Currency, the Federal Reserve Bank, and the FDIC.

Even these safeguards could not prevent the recent failure of the United States Bank in San Diego and of the Franklin National Bank in New York. These two that "went under" were larger than any that failed in the Depression; but due to prompt intervention of banking authorities there was no panic; depositors were protected to the limits of the guarantees; and new investors and capital were found to continue these banking operations under new managements.

Another major change in banking was the introduction of the holding company. Under this device a holding company could acquire, through exchange, the stock of a main operating bank, but, in addition, the holding company could engage in many businesses not permitted to banks: real estate, investment trusts, leasing companies, consumer finance, insurance operations, mortgage companies, factoring, etc. This greater flexibility is supposed to diversify the operation of the business and broaden its horizons of profitability. But it doesn't always work out that way. While many of the big institutions—Citicorp, Chase Manhattan, Wells Fargo, First Chicago, etc.—became successful holding companies, dozens of banks that also followed this course of action would have been better off if they had stuck to their knitting and remained operating banks. Their entry into peripheral activities wound up consuming capital rather than adding to it. In general, the larger metropolitan institutions today are holding companies, with shares listed on NYSE, while most regional and smaller city banks have continued their original status as operating banks, with their shares traded in the OTC market.

Despite any of these associated activities, the primary business of commercial banks is to gather funds on deposit, and loan these funds out to deserving debtors, individual and corporate. These deposits are of two kinds: demand and time. The time type is desirable because the capital remains available to the banks for long periods, although it is necessary to pay interest on these funds. Demand deposits are more mercurial, but banks do not have to pay interest on them. (In 1978, however, many commercial banks introduced plans to pay interest on certain accounts subject to withdrawal by check.) Big metropolitan banks usually attract more demand deposits, while regional and hinterland banks gather more time deposits.

These combined deposits, plus the capital and surplus of a bank and such other funds as it may obtain by sale of preferred stock, or debentures, or by certificates of deposit, provide the total reservoir of assets the bank can draw upon for lending to customers. The procedure is to generate income from the loan portfolio at a higher rate than the money costs. This differential is responsible for most of the gross profits of a bank, before security transactions.

Some supplementary income may be derived from operating a trust department, managing and safekeeping security portfolios, mortgage lending, and renting safe deposit boxes. Further, when economic conditions reduce the demand for loans, banks invest these available funds in securities. Usually government and municipal bonds are used, often of short maturity or with a high degree of marketability, so that monies can be made available on short notice or as demand for loans becomes urgent.

This brings us to an important point in the evaluation of bank stocks. How good are the loans? In the recession period of 1974–75, it turned out that a lot of banks, especially large metropolitan institutions, had gotten careless in their lending and had made sizable loans on real estate and to real estate investment trusts; to owners of oil tankers; and to underdeveloped countries such as Zaire, Zambia, Chile, etc. Defaults occurred on many of these loans and, in 1975 and since, substantial reserves (reducing earnings) had to be set up against possible—in many cases actual—losses in principal and interest. At worst, certain banks charged off as much as 3 percent of average amount in loan portfolio in this way, with a destructive effect on annual earnings. On occasion, a reduction of dividends (as in the case of Marine Midland Bank), or elimination of dividends (as in the case of Citizens and Southern Bank in Atlanta in 1978) resulted.

Accordingly, one of the things you must do in examining quarterly and annual reports of commercial banks is to look at the loan reserve for the year just completed. If this reserve is over .6 of 1 percent of average loan portfolio, it suggests that the bank has not been as vigilant in approving loans as it might have been. Loans made by the bank should be not only "good" (collectible), but profitable. The best-run banks in the country will earn $15 per $1000 on their loan portfolios (namely the net difference between interest charged the customer and the cost of the money lent). Lending money is an enormous business—at 5/15/78 US commercial banks had over $580 billion in their combined loan portfolios.

The profitability of a bank depends not only on interest returns on invested assets, and on the differential between interest received and the cost of money loaned, but also on leverage created by the bank's capitalization. To illustrate, BankAmerica Corporation (the world's largest commercial bank) had average employed assets (calculated at the beginning and end of calendar 1977) of $77,950,778,000. Contrasted with that was the average stockholders' equity of $2,556,399,000. From this, you will note that each $1 of stockholders' equity had over $31 in assets working for it. Putting it another way, shareholders' equity (book value) was only 3.28 percent of assets. This 3.28 percent was among the lowest ratios of assets to equity among major banks. The average figure for 1977 was about 4.5 percent.

Another important ratio in bank share evaluation is the annual return (using income before securities transactions) on stockholders' equity. In the case of BankAmerica, again, this return in 1977 was 15.76 percent. This was among the highest returns of major banks in the country, and substantially above the average of large West Coast banks for the year—13.04 percent. To keep properly liquid, banks are concerned with the ratio of loans to deposits. In 1977, loans among the big institutions averaged around 70 percent. Eighty percent is too high, and BankAmerica's figure for 1977 was 63.1 percent.

A panoramic benchmark of bank profitability is the annual percentage earned on assets. This figure tends to be low for the huge metropolitan banks and higher among the regional and smaller banks. BankAmerica earned .51 percent on average assets employed in 1977, the Rainier Bancorporation in Seattle earned .75 percent and U.S. Bancorp, also on the West Coast, earned 1.05 percent.

Banks are not among the most generous of corporations when it comes to paying dividends. They are, in many instances, so eager to build up capital funds to enable them to lend increasing amounts of money (and thus enhance earning power) that they (especially the elite institutions) set policies of paying around 30 percent of earnings. BankAmerica earned $2.71 a share in fiscal 1977 and paid $.94 in dividends—33 percent.

Banks, however, compensate for rather meager cash dividends by occasional stock dividends and splits, so that shareowners benefit rewardingly in the increase in market value of a larger number of shares. Investors give special recognition to companies that split their shares because some of the most glamorous growth stocks in financial history have split several times (Xerox, Occidental Petroleum, Houston Oil and Minerals, Franklin Life Insurance, etc.).

We have gone to some length to describe bank stocks and the special criteria needed to evaluate them, to enable you to identify potential winners. The annual report of any bank will reveal the ratios we have cited. The final thing we look for is growth—in assets and in per share net, year after year. If an attractive growth rate has been sustained over the past four years (or more) then it may be expected to continue; and the shares may be expected to move higher in market price, partly on the expectation of higher dividends virtually assured by higher earnings.

As to marketability, the biggest bank stocks are listed and traded on NYSE. None are listed on AMEX; but thousands are traded or quoted daily in the OTC market, with volume, bid and asked prices, regularly reported in the over-the-counter section of major metropolitan newspapers.

Big and great as many of these banks are, they have not been among the most popular investments in Wall Street. Most investors never heard of such splendid institutions as Idaho First National Bank or the Central National Corporation chain of banks in Virginia or the Arizona Bank. Everyone of substance, however, should probably own at least one bank stock, and your research in this market sector is bound to lead you to quality securities fully capable of outpacing the DJI.

You should look for bank stocks selling at less than eight times earnings, preferably at or below book value, yielding over 6 percent on present dividends, and earning over 12 percent on book value, with net profits also growing 12 percent or better annually. Identify a bank meeting these criteria, and operating in an area of rising economic stature, and you will locate a serene investment that need not be traded frantically in and out, over short periods of time.

Your opportunity to diversify is splendid. You can select from 14,800 institutions, from very small banks in towns and hamlets to great metropolitan banks with billions on deposit. They're all doing the same things but on different scales—gathering and safeguarding deposits and lending money. The banks that display the most attractive earnings and most dramatic growth are usually found in geographic areas where both population and economic activity are moving briskly ahead. To illustrate, in the past three years most of the standout banks have been located in Florida, the Southwest, the Rocky Mountains, and Pacific states. It has been observed that these sections have sustained their economic forward motion, and were less affected by the 1974–75 recession than other areas. Further, demand deposits (providing the lowest-cost funds for banks to lend) have expanded faster in these sections than time deposits.

Another point to consider is that loan demands, too, can be quite regional, and whereas big New York banks such as Citicorp have suffered from flagging loan demand in 1977–78, many regional and inland banks (serving smaller and local commerce and industry) have been quite fully loaned at excellent rates. In 1979 and 1980, this condition may persist, so that, in selecting bank stocks to "beat the

Dow," we prefer others than the big name banks of New York or Chicago. Not only do we anticipate higher earnings and faster growth rate from regional banks, but we believe perceptive investors will continue to favor them and buy them at modestly rising P/E multiples.

In line with the foregoing benchmarks and criteria for the selection of superior bank shares, on page 107 we present a sample or representative list of issues likely to perform well in the near term future.

The stocks listed in the special selection of bank stocks are representative bank equities of promise. Individual description of 4 banks on the list follows.

## National City Corp.

This bank is spotlighted for its history of outstanding managerial competence. It is a regional industrial city bank, in an area not noted in recent years for outstanding market growth, but it has demonstrated capability to increase its earnings by 10 percent or more annually. It has been increasing its share of the banking market both in Cleveland and statewide; and its earnings for the past six years have grown at an average rate of 12.4 percent. This is the kind of growth that translates into higher dividends and increased market valuation.

Ohio banking laws were changed in 1975, permitting banks to expand by acquiring other banks. National City has made some shrewd acquisitions of high-quality banks, mostly for cash, and has the resources and the managerial capability to continue in this direction.

National City Corp. has no long-term debt; and the ratio

Special selection of Dowbeater bank stocks

| Bank | Earnings Per Share 1976 | Earnings Per Share 1977 | 1977 P/E Ratio | Dividend | % Yield | Nov. 3, 1978 Current Price | 1978–80—% Estimated Growth Rate | Shares Outstanding |
|---|---|---|---|---|---|---|---|---|
| J. P. Morgan & Co. | $5.04 | $5.36 | 8.0 | $2.20 | 4.6 | 47⅝ | 10 | 38,685,000 |
| Alabama Bancorporation | 2.91 | 3.39 | 7.4 | 1.44 | 5.7 | 23 | 12 | 5,838,000 |
| BankAmerica Corp. | 2.40 | 2.71 | 7.7 | .88 | 4.4 | 24⅞ | 11 | 145,697,000 |
| Barnett Banks Fla., Inc. | 1.46 | 1.75 | 9.4 | .88 | 4.6 | 18⅜ | 10 | 8,506,000 |
| Nat'l. City Corp. (Cleveland) | 4.97 | 5.55 | 7.4 | 2.25 | 5.0 | 41 | 10 | 6,924,000 |
| Rainier Bancorporation | 2.87 | 3.29 | 6.8 | .92 | 4.1 | 22 | 12 | 7,487,000 |
| Texas Commerce Bank Shares | 3.33 | 3.85 | 7.8 | 1.22 | 3.5 | 35 | 12 | 9,279,000 |
| The Arizona Bank | 1.54 | 1.84 | 7.3 | .76 | 4.4 | 15¼ | 13 | 3,900,000 |
| **FOR YIELD** | | | | | | | | |
| Wilmington Trust | 5.97 | 6.43 | 5.0 | 2.80 | 8.7 | 32 | 8 | 2,000,000 |
| Chase Manhattan | 2.94 | 3.29 | 9.0 | 2.20 | 7.2 | 30⅝ | 8 | 32,059,000 |
| Philadelphia National | 5.21 | 5.38 | 5.5 | 2.22 | 7.9 | 27¾ | 7 | 5,824,000 |

of shareholders' equity to assets is unusually high, 9.8 percent, compared with 5.7 percent, the average ratio of equity to earning assets for regional banks across the country in 1977. Few banks handle their investment portfolios better than National City. Its municipal portfolio accounted for 23.7 percent of average earning assets in 1977, and yielded above 10 percent.

Cleveland is the core area of the machine tool industry, and the third largest corporate headquarters city in the United States. National City has been doing a good job of expanding its deposits in this corporate milieu, especially demand deposits, the most profitable variety.

In support of the desirability of this stock is the dividend record. Dividends have been increased every year for the past fifteen, the most recent a 9.8 percent increase to $2.25 a share on the 7,900,000 shares outstanding.

Selection of National City Corp. of Cleveland over hundreds of other bank equities has much to justify it.

## The Arizona Bank

Banks in the Sun Belt states have prospered, and The Arizona Bank ranks among the best of them in growth, profitability, and managerial competence. Starting out as The Bank of Bisbee (Arizona) in 1888, in due course this institution, combined with The Bank of Douglas, opened an office in Phoenix (now its headquarters), and opened branches in Tucson, Scottsdale, and Yuma in the 1950s. In 1960 the name was changed (from The Bank of Douglas) to The Arizona Bank, to more accurately describe the stature of the institution and the statewide scope of its operations.

Today The Arizona Bank, with seventy-seven branches, is the largest state-chartered bank in the Rocky Mountain region, and 97th largest US commercial bank, with assets of over $1.3 billion. Between 1971 and 1978 deposits rose from $532 million to $1.1 billion; income before security transactions more than doubled; loans rose from $378 million to $780 million; and stockholders' equity (adjusted for stock splits and dividends to date) from $6.17 to $14.34.

For sixteen years in a row The Arizona Bank has increased its income before security transactions. For 1977 income (excluding profit from sale of office building) was $7,177,850, or $1.84 a share, up from $1.54 per share in 1976. Net chargeoffs, as a percentage of total loans, was .24 percent, contrasted with .69 percent for all US banks with assets between $1 billion and $5 billion. This low ratio is a documentation of superior management. So is 8.94 percent, the average yield on the bank's earnings assets in 1977.

There are 3,900,000 shares outstanding of ABKP (trading symbol in OTC market) with indicated dividend of $.60. Seven stock "extras" have been paid in the past eight years, the latest 15 percent payable 11/28/77. The shares sell below book and below 8 times earnings. ABKP has Dowbeater attributes.

## Alabama Bancorporation

There are six multibank holding companies in Alabama. The largest of these is Alabama Bancorporation, accounting for approximately 14 percent of total commercial deposits in that state. The flagship bank in the system is First National Bank of Birmingham, essentially a wholesale banking institution. The other thirteen banks, rounding out the chain, are essentially consumer banks. The bank has been growing, with respect to earnings, at a rate above 12 percent annually, for the past five years. It appears that this growth rate can be maintained in the years immediately ahead. Growth in earning assets has been at an even faster pace. Quality of the loan portfolio is documented by loan losses which, for the past seven years, have averaged ¼ of 1 percent.

There are 5,838,000 shares outstanding, trading in the OTC market under symbol ABNC. Earnings for some time have returned 14 percent on book value. Dividends have been generous. Cash dividends have been increased in each of the past six years, with payouts ranging 35 to 40 percent of earnings. The stock has been selling around seven times current earnings, and close to its book value.

As the dominant banking institution in a rapidly growing industrial state, ABNC looks attractive and, in the long run, gainful.

## J. P. Morgan & Company, Incorporated

This notable holding company owns Morgan Guaranty Trust Co., the fifth largest bank in the United States and probably the most elite with respect to the quality of its management, its loan portfolio, and the prestige of its clientele. J. P. Morgan is a multi-national and wholesale institution serving the banking needs of large commercial and industrial depositors and of other financial institutions.

The company operates through five offices in New York City, each with complete banking facilities; it also maintains branches or offices in twenty leading cities around the world. A subsidiary holds interests in about forty other banking institutions, worldwide.

Equally competent in domestic and international banking, J. P. Morgan & Company is one of the major dealers in U.S. government bonds and in foreign exchange; it is a leader in corporate lending and has the largest trust department of any commercial bank in America, with over $24 billion in investment assets under its management at the 1977 year end. J. P. Morgan leaves the consumer field to others, and suggests a minimum average balance of $2,000 to individuals opening checking accounts.

The performance of J. P. Morgan is outstanding. Its return on assets is consistently higher than that of competing international banks, and its loss experience is lowest. Over the past five years, the company has increased its net operating income at a 10 percent rate and its dividends at a 7.5 rate. In the five-year period ended December 31, 1977 J. P. Morgan averaged a 15.4 percent return on equity, and an average return on total capital of 12.7 percent—the highest in the industry.

Earnings per share have been in a steady uptrend, rising from $4.96 in 1975 to over $6 in 1978. Capitalization consists of 39,653,366 shares of common stock trading on NYSE under the symbol JPM, preceding by $525.8 million in long-term debt, (including $190 million in convertible debentures). On November 3, 1978, the shares sold at 47⅝ with a $2.50 dividend, and at a P/E multiple of 8. Cash dividends, representing a payout of about 37 percent of net earnings, have been increased frequently. There were 2 for

1 stock splits in 1969 and 1973. Another stock split seems possible in 1979 or 1980. We look for earnings in the range of $6.80 a share in 1979.

In each industry there is usually a "standout" stock: General Motors, IBM, U.S. Steel, AT&T, etc. In banking, the standout issue has to be JPM. In good times or bad, with interest rates high or low, JPM has the ability to glean dependable and rising profits, and to reward its stockholders well.

We have now reviewed the status of commercial banking and the opportunities in that field for making investments, calculated regularly to outpace the DJI. We have also reviewed certain specific stocks with patterns of superior earning power. There are, of course, many other issues that might well be on your shopping list: The Idaho First National Bank, ranking among the best-run institutions in the West; Rainier Bancorp, a progressive bank in Washington State; United Banks of Colorado; Northwest Bancorp, in Minnesota, with over eighty banks in its chain; Texas Commerce Bankshares, one of the most prestigious in Texas; Wachovia Corp., a leading institution in North Carolina; Whitney Holding Corp., an elite bank in New Orleans; Zion Bancorporation in Utah, etc. If you want to invest in the very big banks, then BankAmerica and J. P. Morgan are the standouts.

Because so many fine banks have increased their earnings and dividends regularly over most of the postwar years, stocks in this sector belong in any group of Dowbeaters. Moreover, certain excesses in the banking system—overloaning, overexpanding, and reduced quality of loans—seem to have been corrected. A number of money-center banks have rather fallen from investment favor, probably because such high percentages of their business and profits are "overseas." Citibank, for example, has in recent years derived over half of its net income from operations abroad.

The trends ahead in banking include automatic money transfer, increased consumer banking, broadened use of bank credit cards (VISA), checking against interest-bearing deposits, standby credit lines for individuals, and possibly payment of depositors' bills directly by banks. Electronic fund transfer, which instantly can credit or debit bank accounts, seems to be catching on rather slowly, because people still like the record provided by paying bills by check; and they're suspicious of computerized systems that can foul up and create electronic mazes to be unraveled. Further, it's much harder to "bawl out" a computer than a live bank teller or officer!

We do not expect, however, that technological advances in banking, or even the spread of interstate branch banking, will interfere with the profitability of banking or with gainful investing in bank stocks.

Consider not only the issues we have discussed, but the criteria we have supplied, using them to evaluate those banks in your own community that may have publicly traded shares. Investment in some of them may prove rewarding.

# 9

# Dowbeater
# Bonds

It has always been regarded as prudent to have a backlog of one's investment portfolio in bonds, but since 1974, the attraction of these fixed-income securities has been their high yields. At the US inflation rate peak in late 1974, it was possible to buy AA rated bonds yielding 11 percent, while seasoned stocks were yielding a little over 5½ percent. This income advantage is just too attractive to pass up—a 10 percent or higher return with little or no downside risk, against 5½ percent or below on stocks. So investors are moving in droves into bonds, motivated by the most attractive levels of interest in over a century.

Accordingly today, a representative pension fund contains about 58 percent in bonds and 42 percent in stock—

a reversal of the portfolio ratios prevailing a decade ago. In 1977, an investment in quality bonds would have yielded above 8½ percent against about 5.4 percent for quality stocks, and the stocks would have declined by roughly 17 percent during the year. Such results have sustained the popularity of bonds, both corporate and municipal. The municipals, of course, appeal more to those in upper tax brackets.

Corporate bonds themselves are divided sharply into two major classifications: prime quality and secondary lower-tier obligations (sometimes indelicately referred to in Wall Street as "junk bonds"). We will not dwell at length on the prime quality or investment grade bonds, because these securities have no speculative zing. They are designed primarily to maintain principal values and to assure dependable income with minimum market risk.

But before moving along to the more speculative sector of the bond market, there are a few observations we'd like to make about gilt-edged bonds. Those of investment grade are classified by Moody's into four quality ratings, in descending order: AAA, AA, A, and BAA. If your aim is to salt money away for assured income, then you are urged to make your purchases from these classifications. All these are "safe" bonds. You don't have to analyze or study before purchasing in this area. Just decide on the company, the yield you find acceptable, the maturity desired, and the redemption provisions. The ratings are determined by the stature and stability of the company, the amount of its debt securities, and the number of "times over" interest charges are covered. AAA bonds are, of course, ultrasafe, but there's nothing wrong with BAAs if you can buy them to yield 1 percent higher than AAAs. Further, even among "triple As" there are distinctions. The AAA issues of industrial companies will, in general, yield less than the same rating among utilities because: (1) there are far fewer top-grade industrials available; and (2) utilities are more frequent borrowers and come to Wall Street regularly for the underwriting of additional debt securities. So, with funds at hand, you should probably prefer AAA utilities to similarly graded industrials because of a yield advantage of ¼ percent or more.

So much for the gilt-edged bonds. They are sleek, serene, defensive securities, but not Dowbeaters (except in a bear year!). Moving down the quality ladder (BA and below in the ratings), we enter the arena of secondary bonds, many selling at deep discounts from par value. Here each issue stands by itself, and ratings are traditionally lowly and sometimes quite unflattering.

In considering these issues for gainful investment there are two things to remember: theoretically, the ultimate market trend of every discount bond is upward toward par at maturity; and even if a bond defaults on its interest or principal, the situation is not entirely hopeless. There are usually significant corporate assets available to meet claims of bondholders at least in part; and in many instances, ensuing reorganizations have resulted in the issuance of new securities which, over a period of time, restored original par value, or even more, to patient holders. Remember also that secondary bonds pay high yields (current interest divided by price) and that their appreciation in value, above the (discount) price you pay, is treated (if a long-term holding) as a capital gain, for tax purposes. Furthermore, you can borrow on the bonds, and the return on them may exceed the interest you pay on the loan that finances their purchase.

If you are interested in high yields and have the fortitude to accept erratic market swings, you may do well in "junk" bonds. Regard them, however, less as bonds than as common stocks with coupons, because indeed some, at the lowest tier, are very risky and have to struggle to make each interest payment. Most of them are pretty likely to survive, however, if a general upturn in the economy is in sight, and if continued inflation makes debt and interest charges more tolerable.

The factors that will make lower-tier bonds go up are: (1) declining interest rates (which are bullish for all kinds of bonds); (2) an upturn in the earning power of the issuing company; (3) a new management or "takeover"; (4) generation of sufficient corporate funds (or bank borrowing) to "buy in" bonds at deep discounts (creating debt reduction and an attractive gain in corporation net worth); (5) a powerful upswing in the company's common stock, if the issue is convertible; and (6) notable enhancement of total corporate assets, such as an oil property or mineral claim holding proved valuable by exploratory drilling.

Success in these submerged bonds will come by buying at the right time and at deep discounts, in companies that present reasonable survival characteristics and that may benefit by upturns in their industry, or by a rapid general expansion in the economy. One buys such bonds with mixed emotions: you like the high current yields (50 to 100 percent over savings-account rates), even though there is always lurking the possibility of a default; you like the idea of buying $3000 par of bonds for $2000, or, better yet, $2000 of bonds for $1000. (You can do that now—November 3, 1978 —with Cenco Inc.'s 5's of 1996 selling at 48.) The theory is that the generous yield and the price appreciation hoped for may earn 30 to 50 percent on your money in a year. If the Cenco bond, for example, moves to 65 and you sell, your realization will be $50 in interest and $150 in capital gain, a total of $200, which is 40 percent on the $500 you staked.

To illustrate the opportunities in low-priced bonds here are some examples culled from the New York Stock Exchange bond list in mid-November 1978. There is not a whisper of recommendation or endorsement about any of these issues, and you should get a late earnings report on each before even thinking of making any commitment.

| Issue | % Coupon | Maturity | Nov. 3, 1978 Price | % Current Yield |
|---|---|---|---|---|
| Budget Capital | 6 | 2010 | 54 | 11.1 |
| General Host | 7 | 1994 | 60 | 11.6 |
| Jones & Laughlin Steel | 6¾ | 1994 | 67 | 10.0 |
| Rapid American (6) | 7 | 1994 | 52⅜ | 13.5 |
| White Motor | 7¼ | 1993 | 55⅞ | 12.8 |
| Wisconsin Central RR | 4 | 2004 | 52⅛ | 7.7 |
| Missouri Pacific RR | 5 | 2045 | 56½ | 7.7 |
| Telex | 9 | 1996 | 76 | 11.9 |

Most of these are unsecured debentures. Wisconsin Central and Missouri Pacific are 'income" bonds; that is, they pay interest in any year only if it is earned. (Unpaid interest, however, accrues.) All of these bonds are currently covering their interest charges except the Chase Manhattan Mortgage issue, which is the subordinated note of a rather troubled real estate investment trust. The Missouri Pacific bond is due far enough in the future (A.D. 2045) so that we don't need to worry about payment at maturity.

Next, we move along to another beckoning sector of the bond market—convertible bonds. These, like most of the issues in the above table, are debentures but they have a "kicker"; they are all convertible into the common stock of their respective companies. In every instance the conversion privilege is today of no value, and profitable conversion seems miles away; but still it could occur. You might call these "sunburned" convertibles. Here's a random shopping list of "converts."

| Issue | % Coupon | Maturity | Current Price Nov. 3, 1978 | % Current Yield | # of Shares per Bond | Stock Price |
|---|---|---|---|---|---|---|
| Alexanders Inc. | 5½ | 1996 | 53½ | 10.1 | 31.01 | 5¾ |
| Cenco Inc. | 5 | 1996 | 48 | 10.4 | 43.01 | 4 |
| Eastern Air Lines | 5 | 1992 | 59½ | 8.0 | 20.00 | 9⅝ |
| Fedders Corp. | 5 | 1996 | 48¼ | 10.3 | 20.00 | 4¾ |
| National Homes | 4¾ | 1996 | 40¼ | 11.3 | 24.10 | 2¾ |
| Pan American World Airways | 5¼ | 1989 | 60½ | 8.8 | 48.57 | 7½ |
| Ramada Inns | 5 | 1996 | 70¼ | 7.0 | 58.65 | 9⅛ |
| United Brands | 5½ | 1994 | 58½ | 9.3 | 18.18 | 9⅛ |
| U.S. Steel | 5¾ | 2001 | 71 | 8.0 | 15.94 | 23⅜ |
| Zayre Corp. | 5¾ | 1994 | 64 | 9.0 | 25.00 | 11½ |

Obviously, the common stocks of these companies will have to perform miracles if these bonds are to benefit. But regardless of the remoteness of profitable conversion, the possibility is there. These "converts" have more potential "zing" than "straight" debentures because of this possible future feature.

Just by way of illustration, Budd Co., an unromantic maker of railway and transit cars, has a "convert," the 5⅞ percent debentures due 1994, selling in 1976 at $580. These were (and are) convertible into 45.23 shares of Budd common. However, in January 1978, a German firm emerged that wanted to take over Budd at $36 a share. All of a sudden this tired conversion option had real value, and the bonds zoomed up to $1460 each on February 1, 1978.

If you've got real sporting blood you might want to take on a few lower-tier convertibles. If so, follow the company's earnings like a hawk.

Finally, we reach the very bottom drawer of junk bonds: those that have already defaulted. Here the name of the game is patience, while you wait, month after month, for a reorganization plan to be approved by a court—a plan that may give you $.20 to $.40 on the dollar in fixed income securities, and possibly a package of new preferred or common stock; and sometimes warrants. Meanwhile, the bond will fluctuate and you are deprived of any current interest or dividend return. For the patient, however, defaulted securities may be rewarding. Many individuals who bought defaulted rail bonds in 1933–37 cleaned up profits of 200 and 300 percent.

Again, here's a random shopping list of very tired defaulted bonds:

| Issue | % Coupon | Maturity | Price |
|-------|----------|----------|-------|
| American Export | 5¼ | 1993 | 15 |
| Chicago Mil. RR | 4 | 1994 | 38½ |
| Guardian Mortgage | 7½ | 1979 | 38 |
| N.Y. Central | 4 | 2013 | 37 |

The railway bonds have first mortgage property liens; the American Export 5¼s are convertible (but who cares) and the Guardian 7½s are (you'll pardon the expression) secured notes. All have a long way to go. Keep on the lookout for companies declaring bankruptcy such as United Manufacturers recently, and several REITs in wobbly condition. Time and an improved economy may bring them back to life. Barnett-Winston 8¼ percent debentures are the sort of thing you might want to investigate.

If you are serious about designing a portfolio of secondary bonds: (1) diversify—spread your risks over four or five different issues; (2) get current reports on company earnings and watch for any improvement (or deterioration) in interest coverages; (3) watch interest rates. If interest rates are going down, your bonds, however lowly in stature, also have a better chance to go up.

Few individuals hold "junk" bonds to maturity. They prefer to trade in and out, selling an issue that has made a sizable profit and looking around for another bond at a deep discount to replace it. Well timed, a program of investment in junk bonds can be rewarding. Your goal is 30 to 50 percent appreciation in a year—and that in most cases will "beat the Dow."

Finally, don't confine your selection to "listed" bonds.

There are dozens of tired industrial and realty bonds trading over the counter. Search for and select an interesting value and then put in a bid for a few bonds—and wait. Don't get "itchy" and reach up for faded bonds. You can, by exercising patience, often get them at close to your original target price. Later on, the company itself may make an offer to buy in a certain number of bonds at a fixed price. Weigh such an offer carefully. It may "bail you out" at a profit but, after all these bonds have been "bought in" and retired, the remaining bonds will be in a stronger position and have better interest coverage.

Actually, the whole security market is very lopsided, composed, in total, of over 80 percent in bonds outstanding, and only 20 percent in equity securities. But "the action" is mostly in the equities!

We recommend that you buy prime bonds for contentment, second-tier bonds for high income plus appreciation, and defaulted bonds as long-shot speculations, or for sheer adventure!

# PART FOUR
# DOWBEATER
# SPECULATIONS

# Profits in
# Takeovers

In a book designed to winnow out from the general run of stocks those able not only to outperform the DJI but possibly to double within two years, some attention should surely be paid to acquisition and mergers. Indeed, some of the most rapid and substantial capital gains in the markets of 1976–8 were in takeover stocks. A number of "target" issues advanced 75 to 100 percent in a matter of weeks, as bidding for them became hotly contested.

The classic case in 1977 was Babcock and Wilcox. In March 1977, this stock was minding its own business, modestly trading around $35. Out of the blue came United Technologies, with a takeover bid of $42. Then J. Ray McDermott & Co. got into the act and began buying shares in the open market. United Technologies raised the ante to $48. McDermott raised to $55 and finally to $65 a share to buy enough B & W shares to give it 49 percent. The B & W management had disfavored becoming part of United Technologies and had set up legal obstacles against UT, regarding McDermott as a more desirable and acceptable purchaser.

Stockholders in B & W made more money on their shares within a few weeks than they had for some years earlier. From $35 to $65 is almost 90 percent! Stockbrokers prospered on the deal, too, through heavy daily trading volume; and the investment bankers (and lawyers) who counseled the companies pocketed fees that made negotiated commission business look mousy!

This contest for ownership and control was no isolated phenomenon. Mergers and acquisitions in 1976 amounted to more than $20 million and aggregated close to $18 billion in 1977. The big year, however, was 1969, with a grand total of $24 billion involved. The takeover boom may now be slowing down a bit, perhaps because so many natural "quarries" have already been absorbed. In the 1980s we may expect many more mergers, but they will probably be fewer in number than currently, and involve bigger companies.

Before we arrive at specific ideas on where to look for merger stocks that may outperform "the Dow" it might be well to examine motivations. Why does a substantial corporation desire to buy out another for cash? Why is it willing to pay a premium over the historic price range, in which the target issue had been trading? Why not use that money to build a new plant, to improve or add to existing capital equipment? The best answer to those questions is that it's cheaper to buy than to build! Indeed, for many companies loaded with cash, a takeover may be one of the best investments it can make.

The identification of a takeover candidate usually starts with its financial statements. If these reveal a strong cash position, modern and well-maintained equipment, and a stock selling at a low multiple and well below its book value, then a company becomes attractive. A record of stable and preferably rising earnings and sales is also desirable.

The company under consideration may fit in well with the acquisitor's main line of business (as when International Nickel absorbed ESB, a maker of storage batteries, or Pepsico took over Pizza Hut). The target may have a stodgy and tired management so that injection of a new executive team might dramatically improve its earning power. Sometimes the motivation is either to diversify or flatten out the cyclical nature of the acquisitor's business, or to provide entry into an entirely new field. The latter was the case when Mobil took over Marcor. Moving into a new industrial sector may also seem desirable if a traditional business is phasing out, or operating at steadily declining profit margins.

The name of the game is to earn profit, whether in your own line or someone else's. If the target corporation's shares sell below "book," and the company is earning 10 to 12 percent on invested capital and growing at a rate of 8 to 10 percent annually, it becomes worth considering. In general, the buyer wants to purchase below stockholders' equity because it must write off any price excess over book value (good will) over a period of no longer than forty years. Any such "writeoff" reduces reported profits.

Companies that make takeovers today seem willing to pay, on the average, 60 to 70 percent higher than earlier quotations for a stock (1) to be sure they get the company, (2) to shake out reluctant sellers, (3) to get their hands on a cash-rich balance sheet, (4) because book value may be grossly understated and the properties of the target company could not now be duplicated for double or treble their depreciated values, (5) to get a "hot" management team or instant penetration of a desired market. If a company decides to enter the convenience-food industry, for example, it can do so more economically by buying a company already entrenched in that field than by starting from scratch.

Just because there have been so many mergers and there's a headline on the financial page about a new one almost daily does not mean they are easy to complete. No, indeed. First, the target company may not want to be acquired (most don't). It may defend by hiring attorneys, getting friends and employees to buy more stock, employing an investment house as consultant, soliciting proxies, and advertising in the financial press. Also, there are now antitakeover laws in thirty-one states that may impede or block a merger. A reluctant company may also invoke antitrust laws or call upon regulatory agencies such as the SEC to intervene. Such tactics as these may delay a merger or impose so many roadblocks and legal and accounting expenses that "the wolf" will go away.

Finally a company, helpless against invasion, may look around to find a friendlier wolf. When Occidental Petroleum sought to take over Kern County Land a few years back, the Kern management was unhappy at the prospect of being run by Occidental. Within weeks a newfound brother, Tenneco, Inc., was approached and persuaded to take over Kern. Occidental lost out, but did make a few millions in capital gains on the sale of the Kern stock it had purchased along the way.

Incidentally, it is almost standard operating procedure

for an acquiring company to buy a chunk of target stock (maybe 5 or 10 percent) before trundling out its big guns.

It has become an important divisional operation of several big Wall Street firms to search for takeover candidates, to structure strategic mergers, and to help find new suitors if the first one is disliked; and to calculate the offering prices most likely to win properties and to "keep out the grocery clerks." The majors in this field would include Morgan Stanley & Co., Goldman Sachs & Co., Kidder Peabody, Solomon Bros., Lazard Freres, Lehman Brothers, First Boston, and White Weld, etc.

As long as the prices of common stocks remain relatively low and with prevailing P/E multiples of 9 or 10 (preferably lower), and so long as there are dozens of publicly held companies around with earning assets very costly to replace (but reasonably priced for acquisition) and big companies with plenty of surplus cash, you'll continue to see a parade of merger proposals. (Where no other companies appear that are attractive, the next best thing to do seems to be to buy in your own stock, as IBM, Tandy, Teledyne, Mite Corp., etc., have done.)

The recent scripts of acquisitions is impressive: General Electric took over Utah International; Unilever bought National Starch & Chemical; Arco won Anaconda Copper; International Tel. and Tel. acquired Eason and Carbon Industries; Kennecott offered what seemed a gaudy price ($66 a share) for Carborundum; Allegheny Ludlum took Chemetron; Union Carbide added Amchen Products; Nestlé Products (Switzerland) acquired Alcon Laboratories. Takeover bids don't always prevail, however. In 1977 Sambos Restaurant, Koehring, Western Publishing, and Applied Digital

Data were all wooed. Their stocks bounced up on the rumors, but no takeovers occurred.

Somewhat related to takeovers is the phenomenon we mentioned above—a company buying its own shares in the open market or making a tender offer. This, too, is of interest to investors in quest of capital gains. When a company has developed a rich cash flow and strong current balance-sheet position, and decides not to make acquisitions, it may choose to spend some of its surplus funds buying in its own stock. Many companies have been doing this in recent years, the classic example being IBM, which laid out $700 million to buy its shares at $280.

Why should a company buy its stock, engaging in what Wall Street calls "corporate cannibalism?" There are several pretty plausible reasons:

1. To reduce the number of outstanding shares and by so doing increase the earnings and dividends per share accruing to the remaining equity.
2. To satisfy stockholders who may have complained that their shares weren't getting sponsorship.
3. To provide a measure of market support in the issue when general interest in it is lagging.
4. To express confidence in the desirability of its own shares.
5. To have treasury shares available for pension, or bonus plans, or to be offered in a desired merger.
6. To buy in at a low multiple. If a company buys in stock at five times earnings, it is making 20 percent on its money.

The objections to the practice are that (1) growing companies should be seeking more stockholders and wider distribution of shares rather than contracting the amount of stock in public hands; (2) larger cash dividends on outstanding stock would please shareowners and motivate market action better; (3) a well-managed company should use its cash to expand earning assets, enter new product lines, and engage in forward-looking research rather than limit or reduce the scope of its operations.

In actual practice, we are not aware of instances where a company's announcement of a stock repurchase has zoomed its shares, although it may have prevented them from declining further. In any event a takeover rumor or announcement is far more likely to product a swift capital gain for you than a program of treasury stock buying.

From the foregoing, we conclude that there exist quite frequently opportunities for short-run capital gains stemming from takeover talk or rumors to firm cash bids for particular issues. Once mentioned, a stock that might have been languishing for months at a so-so price begins to attract a following, and previous valuations of the issue are revised upward in light of its newly found "merger bait" characteristics. Volume in the issue expands and traders have no difficulty moving in and out, on attractive interim swings.

If you acquire shares of the target company as soon as the rumor surfaces, your chances of gain become excellent and chances of loss minimal. The subject stock is almost certain to enter a new and higher market orbit. Among the best performers of 1977 were takeover candidates such as Carborundum, American Medicorp, Miles Laboratories, and National Starch & Chemical.

To illustrate the importance of early entry into a merger situation observe the market action in two representative instances. Miles Laboratories hadn't shown much animation and was trading at $25 when management announced that merger discussions were in progress. That release was sufficient to push the shares up to $29. Next the buyer, Bayer A.G., a major German industrial company, announced it would pay up to $40 a share, and when shareowners were languid in their response, increased the offer to $47, ultimately the winning price.

Alcon Laboratories was selling at 25 when a large Swiss buyer, Nestlé S.A., surfaced and later announced a tender offer of $42, which on November 21, 1977 propelled the shares to 41⅝. In both of these cases, investors were shown a fairly clear highway to rewarding profits. Even when takeover announcements do not materialize, the target stocks usually behave reasonably well, and make money for those who bought on the first press release. Merger bait shares generally sell in higher price ranges, even after a takeover bid that didn't jell.

If there are competitors, instead of just one buyer on the horizon, so much the better. American Medicorp, like the Babcock & Wilcox case, illustrates the benefits of competitive striving. Humana, another hospital company, was all set to take over American Medicorp at around $15 a share in stock when TWA, with its Hilton International subsidiary, came up with a better offer, $20 a share in cash. AM rose in 1977 from $8 to $21¼, a gain of 165 percent.

Merger negotiations place special obligations on corporate officers and directors. First, they must publicly disclose the possibility of takeover as promptly as possible, lest stockholders sell stock in ignorance and sue management for profits lost due to nondisclosure of important information. Second, officers are not supposed to benefit from "inside information." For example, they may not, in good conscience, buy more of their own stock on the strength of an attractive merger bid in the offing. Equally, the management of the acquiring company is expected (1) to publicly announce its intentions as promptly as possible, (2) to inform its own stockholders, and (3) not to buy stock in the target company in the knowledge that a higher price will ultimately be paid for it. This is the age of stockholder suits and class actions, so officials must be honorable and discreet, if only to avoid lawsuits!

While most recent takeovers have been for cash, the tax-free exchange of securities is still desirable in many cases, although wide swings in the prices of the stocks involved may cause exchange offers to be modified or withdrawn. Also some acquirers have grown impatient with managements that drag their feet in accepting a cash offer, and have on occasion reduced the tender price, or threatened to do so, to accelerate a decision. This may also place blame on officers and directors for their failure to accept or act upon an attractive offer, and might lead to a stockholders' suit, if the final offer were less than a rejected earlier offer.

In any event, it is decidedly worthwhile for investors to keep alert to possible mergers because the gains for early birds can be swift and substantial, and the risks of loss quite low. As soon as you read about a possible buyout on the financial pages, or see it announced on a news ticker, investigate. If the company sought has a good earning record for three prior years, a sound balance sheet, well-regarded products or services, if its stock is thinly held by management, and if management has appeared inept and unimaginative, the company will probably be snapped up, and you'd better get aboard. If a big, well-run company such as Marcor or Carborundum is up for grabs, the acquirer has to be a strong, well-heeled company, and the profits from early purchase of the quarry shares seem well assured. The only people who are willing to pay well "over market" for stocks recently are expanding companies—or Arabs! The buyers today are much stronger than the conglomerate traders of the 1960s, and they are building sturdier corporate clusters and stronger capitalizations.

Finally, as a rough roadmap to future merger profits, here is a random list of possible takeover candidates:

| | | |
|---|---|---|
| Norton Co. | St. Joe Paper | Varo, Inc. |
| Cenco | Sharon Steel | Durham Life Insurance |
| Morton-Norwich | General Cable | |
| Curtis-Wright | Reichold Chemicals | Wrather Corp. |
| Dome Mines | Affiliated Hospitals | Amdahl Corp. |
| Florida East Coast | Electronic Research | Burnup & Sims |
| Kennecott | McCulloch Oil | Hartford Steam Boiler |
| Rapid American | Shenandoah Oil | |
| Foremost-McKesson | Terradyne | Pizza Inn |
| Hecla Mining | Wolverine Shoe | Rival Mfg. |
| Fred S. James | Sea Services | Velcro Industries |
| Mattel | McAndrews & Forbes | Asarco |
| National Mine Service | | Associated Coca-Cola |
| General American Oil | Zayre | |

One clue you can get to possible takeover is an existing minority investment. Many of the companies listed above are already partially owned by possible acquirers.

Watch these and many others and you may cash in on the merger. Always buy the takeover stock, not that of the wolf!

# ⊓⊓

# "All That Glitters
# Is Not Gold"

## Silver as Gainful Investment

Copper was the first metal to be mined by man, and worked
into useful utensils, around 6000 B.C. Next on the historic
scene came gold and silver—attractive, exciting, and desirable because of their luster, divisibility, malleability, dura-
bility, and relative scarcity. Both have always been avidly
acquired by the rich and ruling classes in skillfully crafted
earrings, bracelets, necklaces, rings, bowls, knives, and cups
to evidence their status and opulence. These precious metals
were also used to adorn the graves of departed nobility, so
that they might eternally bask in an environment of luxury.

As water transportation developed, peoples living hundreds of miles apart began trading with each other. Barter-

ing for goods became customary—swapping so many bushels of wheat for an Oriental rug. But this method of marketing was unwieldy and eager traders in many lands early recognized the need for a uniform and convenient medium of exchange that could simplify trading, be widely and readily acceptable to both buyers and sellers, and represent a standard and a store of value. After experimenting with all sorts of commodities—grain, salt, cattle, sheep, shells, olive oil, land, dates, and even people—man found that metals made the best media of exchange. Of all the metals tried, gold and silver were found the most satisfactory. At first, these were used as crude money in bars or rings, but these forms were clumsy, not uniform in weight, and their values were uncertified.

These monetary problems were solved by a famous and exceedingly rich potentate, King Croesus of Lydia. He invented the coinage of money in 560 B.C. and minted coins in both gold and silver about the size and shape of a lima bean. Each coin carried the figures of a bear and a lion stamped on the reverse side. Minted coins have been internationally accepted as money ever since.

The most valuable and important coins, over the centuries, were of gold: the daric of Persia, the dinar of the Arab world, the aureus of Rome, the ducat of Venice, the florin of Florence, the Napoleon of France, the sovereign of England, the Spanish doubloon, and the gold eagles of the United States. The more common coins used in small daily transactions, however, have traditionally been of silver: the denarius of Rome, the French franc, the British shilling, and American dimes, quarters, halves, and dollars (minted of 90 percent silver until 1965).

Both gold and silver have thus served important roles as monetary metals, but these have been reduced somewhat in importance during the past century by the increasing use of paper currencies, and especially by checking accounts and money substitutes such as credit cards. All along the way, however, both gold and silver have been increasingly used in jewelry and ornamentation. In the twentieth century, industrial applications of both metals have notably expanded demands. Gold is used in dentistry, as insulation, in electronics, and most recently in a film as insulation against heat or cold for plate-glass windows in office buildings. Silver has been effectively applied to several major industrial uses that have created whole new markets for that metal. And continuously over centuries, as depressions, inflations, and devaluations of currencies have occurred in many nations, individuals have acquired and hoarded gold and silver in coin, bar, and jewelry to preserve their wealth and maintain their buying power.

In recent years hoarding of (or investment in) these precious metals has notably affected their prices, particularly since August 15, 1971, when America went off the gold standard. Since then, all the major currencies of the world have been "floating" in kaleidoscopic price relationships with each other. How long this floating of exchange rates will last, and whether or not we shall, in due course, return to a currency backed by gold, is not a major topic in this book. We are concerned, however, with the investment merits of these metals because they remain scarce and both appear in long-term price uptrends as inflation remains rampant around the world.

Gold is indeed scarce, with only 83,000 metric tons in

existence above ground and global mining producing only about 1350 new tons a year. Gold has had some dramatic price moves: from $35 an ounce in 1968 to a high of $197.50 in December 1974; back to $103 an ounce in August 1976; then slowly working back up to $245.25 in October 1978. Those swings created several profit opportunities in coins, bullion, and the stocks of gold-mining companies.

Our view, however, is that in the next decade silver is likely to outperform gold. Why? Because, for over twenty years, the free world's demand for silver has substantially exceeded the production of newly mined silver, and silver is increasingly in demand worldwide by industrial users and by investors and hoarders.

Historically, as mentioned, the major uses of silver were in currency, ornamentation, and tableware for the dining rooms of the civilized world. But since World War II, the annual demand for silver has been massively boosted by technological advances in the photographic and electronics industries. In fact, total demand has far exceeded the production of new silver from the mines of the noncommunist world. This gap has comprised 100 million ounces for several years, and has resulted in a steady erosion of existing stores worldwide. The deficiency has been filled by silver sold from the US stockpile, recycled from scrap (mainly the film industry), sales by individuals, melting down of coins, and inflow of silver from India and Pakistan (mostly melted-down jewelry).

This progressive silver shortage continues, and is apt to continue. We are unlikely to fill this gap from mining, since most of the great mines of silver (near the earth's surface) have been exhausted and few new "pure" silver mines are being developed. Moreover, 75 percent of new silver production around the world is derived as a byproduct from the mining of lead, copper, and zinc. In the past three years, production of these base metals has not increased, and whatever gains in silver mining have occurred have come from a very few new pure silver mines coming on stream: Coeur d'Alene in Idaho and Lacana in Mexico, for example.

For many decades prior to 1870, progressive nations around the world freely coined silver bullion presented at their mints, and for much of the nineteenth century the US Treasury had a steady silver price of $1.29 an ounce. However, greatly expanded silver production at the time of the Comstock Lode in Nevada, coupled with reduction of silver minting and the end of bimetallism in many countries (after 1871), set silver on an entirely new course. On-and-off government support of the domestic silver industry motivated erratic price swings.

The Bland-Allison Silver Purchase Act of 1878 called for government purchase of $4 million worth of silver a month to be minted into silver dollars (a sop to the "silver states"); but it didn't cause silver to rise in price. It was only $.92 an ounce in 1888. After the United States adopted an exclusive gold standard in 1900, silver dropped as low as $.47, in 1902. It was $.67 in 1918 and reached a postwar top of $1.37 an ounce in 1919.

The next milestone for silver was the Thomas Amendment, passed in 1933, that enabled debtor countries to pay the United States off in silver valued at $.50 an ounce (a premium allowance above the Depression low price of $.25

an ounce). Nationalization of silver in 1934 closed the silver commodity trading exchanges and a series of treasury "floor" prices kept the market low for years ($.35 in 1939).

Then there ensued a slow price uptrend to $.71 in 1945, to $1.20 in 1962, and in due course to $1.29 in 1963—a Treasury-controlled price representing a 28 to 1 ratio between silver and gold. The year 1965 was the last time that US coinage of silver was made in the ratio of 90 percent silver to 10 percent base metal; and 320 million ounces were used for US minting that year.

Two years later, the Treasury could no longer stabilize the metal at an official coinage price of $1.293. In 1967, the Treasury introduced cupro-nickel quarters and dimes, and used 54 million ounces of silver to strike Kennedy half-dollars (40 percent silver). Silver coins struck before 1966 became collectors' items and disappeared from daily use, selling at good premiums over face value because they became worth far more "melted up" than as legal tender.

The Treasury liquidated a stock of over two billion ounces of silver in the early 1970s. Silver sold at $1.75 in 1967, peaked at $2.56 in June 1968, then reacted to $1.80, depressed by frequent Treasury auctions. The low was $1.34 in late 1971. Since then, silver has tended to follow the price of gold up. Silver reached $3 in 1973, and zoomed to an all-time high of $6.70 in February 1974. Then it receded, trading below $4 in 1975. Since that low, the supplies below the $6 level for silver have been snapped up, and silver is ready for a move to all-time highs.

Today the historical ratio of silver to gold is at an extreme level. We believe that this ratio is about to change in favor of silver. Silver is still a sleeper, with most silver stocks just emerging from years of dormancy. This has occurred while millions of inflation-crazed investors sought haven in gold stocks.

With these factors in mind, and the fact that just a minor price rise in silver will ignite a major earnings upheaval in silver stocks, the time is right to initiate positions in silver stocks or to switch gold stocks into silver stocks. The following requirements are essential for finding the right silver mines for you: (1) the quality and extent of silver ore bodies owned or controlled (prefer long-life mines); (2) the nearness of the mine to "civilization" (reducing costs of labor and transportation); (3) capability of the management; (4) efficiency of mining and milling operations; (5) access of management to additional capital which may be required for further exploration or development of ore bodies or to build or enlarge a mill or concentrator.

The merits of mining shares are their convenience, marketability, potential for gain, a return in the form of dividends (coins, bullion, and futures pay nothing), and finally, a long-term call on metal still in the ground. If the price of silver soars, then shares in proven mining companies should be profit-prone. Here are the stocks we recommend as representative of good silver mining investments:

Texasgulf, Inc., is not only one of the world's largest producers of sulfur, but a major producer of copper as well. In connection with its copper production from a rich mine in Timmins, Ontario, it turned out a record 10,555,000 ounces of silver in 1974 (less since), making it Canada's largest silver producer. TG has 30,477,477 common shares outstanding, quoted on NYSE at 20 on October 27, 1978. Here again is an interesting metal stock wherein silver output is secondary to and determined by production of base metals.

On the international scene is Rosario Resources, which appears attractive with a rich mine, Pueblo Viejo, in the Dominican Republic (27 percent owned) that can turn out 1,500,000 ounces of silver and 380,000 ounces of gold per year. Other mining properties are in Nicaragua, with large silver production in Mexico from its own mines and those of the Fresnillo Company (producing together over four million ounces a year) acquired in 1977. Rosario (ROS) has 5,990,000 shares on NYSE and sold at 18⅝ on November 3, 1978.

Sunshine Mining can turn out 4 million ounces of silver in a good year, but the property has been hampered by strikes, a fire, and a bickering management. In 1977 a controlling interest in the property was acquired by the wealthy Hunt family in Texas, and improved earnings are expected from the property in the future. Nobody is more bullish on silver than the Hunts. There are 5,617,018 common shares of Sunshine listed on NYSE (symbol, SSC), selling on November 3, 1978 at 11⅜.

Another representative silver entry is Callahan Mining, with a 50 percent interest in the pretax cash flow of Galena Mine (silver, copper) in Idaho, operated by Asarco. The mine can produce 2.2 million ounces of silver annually. There are 3,462,706 shares of CMN listed on NYSE selling at 14 on November 3, 1978.

Day Mines, with 2,964,866 shares listed on AMEX (trading symbol DMI), deserves consideration as another significant producer in the Coeur d'Alene district in Idaho and leaseholder on the substantial silver-lead mining property of

Leadville Corp., Leadville, Colorado. DMI traded on November 3, 1978 at 10½.

Other US silver shares you might consider are Hecla Mining (primarily in copper and financially troubled) and Coeur d'Alene, a new mine in Idaho whose shares trade in the OTC market (around 10).

United Keno, an important Canadian silver mine, is located way up in the Yukon Territory. It has been a fine producer and earner but its ore reserves have been running low, so we don't particularly favor it.

An interesting Canadian company is Agnico-Eagle Mines, unique in that it is the only mining company of stature in Canada devoted exclusively to gold and silver production.
It produces around 80,000 ounces of gold and 400,000 ounces of silver a year. Silver production is believed on the increase because of its location of new ore bodies by drilling to greater depth in some older mines in the Cobalt district of Ontario.

Agnico-Eagle should have a cash flow of about $2,900,000 in 1978 and has been allocating a good percentage of this to expanding its gold orebody at the Eagle Mine, Joutel, Quebec. Agnico-Eagle has 13,862,000 shares outstanding listed on Toronto Exchange and trading in the OTC market in the United States. The company has some 25,000 stockholders, and should be in line for dividends in 1979, selling at 4⅝ in Toronto on November 3, 1978.

Another attractive silver stock is Lacana Mining Corp., a Canadian company with its principal properties in Mexico. From the six mines brought on stream in the past decade, 1977 production was approximately 3 million ounces of silver, 22 million pounds of lead, and 12,000 ounces of gold.

Earnings of above $.35 a share seem possible in 1978. The principal production properties are four mines and a 2000-ton-per-day concentrator making up the Torres Mining complex near Guanajuato, Mexico. Lacana shares a 30 percent interest in this along with Fresnillo (now part of Rosario) 37 percent and Penoles S.A. 33 percent. This mining complex cost $43 million to put into production. Lacana supplements its earnings from Torres by Encantada Mines (40 percent owned) in Northern Mexico, capable of producing 2,700,000 ounces of silver and 55 million pounds of lead annually.

Other properties include a gold mine in Nevada, 30 percent of an extensive uranium property in British Columbia, and other projects in Canada, Guatemala, and Costa Rica.

There are, after the 1977 offering of 1,500,000 shares and 750,000 warrants to buy Lacana at up to $4.50 a share until 12/15/81 by Wood, Gundy & Co. in Toronto, 8,835,316 shares of Lacana outstanding, trading on Toronto Exchange and OTC in the United States. About 17 percent of Lacana stock is owned by DuPont of Canada. Shares sold at 4⅞ in Toronto on November 3, 1978.

These silver mines are all attractive speculations. They all have significant reserves in the ground that will surface only with substantially higher silver prices in the eighties. Buy and hold!

# 12

# Lazarus Securities:
# Stocks to Come Up
# from the Dead

The trouble with Wall Street in recent years is that most of the zest and adventure have been removed. Today's "players" seem meekly content to lodge most of their surplus funds in 9½ percent bonds, mutual funds of all descriptions, traditional common stocks for fixed income, balanced funds, municipal bonds, growth and energy, etc. These may all be reasonably prudent vehicles for the deployment of money, but most are geared primarily to safety of principal and comfortable yields. They are quite devoid of any speculative zing or possibility of exciting expectation of gain in market prices.

With 70 percent of all transactions on the Big Board now executed for institutional accounts, and with pension and welfare funds totaling over $400 billion, the portfolio accent is heavily on large, seasoned companies with millions of outstanding listed shares. Probably at no time in Wall Street history has there been so little effort expended in an eager quest for high-percentage capital gains.

Toward that objective, this chapter examines a sector of the market that is the native habitat of shares generating the most explosive market action. These lower-priced issues can move up and down with pace and animation, and since 1968 they have been woefully neglected by brokerage firms and investors. People with market funds seem to have lost their sporting blood. Why? Because of the solemn institutionalization of investment procedures; because of significant structural changes that have taken place within the securities business; and finally because, since 1968, speculators in general have not made out very well, and market "killings" have been few and far between.

Consider the changes in the machinery of Wall Street within the past decade. Firms have disappeared in droves. Many formerly well-known NYSE brokerage houses have gone out of business or have merged for survival purposes. There are now 470 member firms on the NYSE, as compared to 684 in 1961. Those firms that remain have contracted their sales forces and notably reduced their research departments. Thus, today the number of security issues regularly "covered" by exchange firms has been greatly contracted and the stress, in both research and sales, is heavily on seasoned blue chips and traditional "glamour" issues; or on companies with which the larger firms maintain continuing investment banking relationships.

Consequently, thousands of substantial companies with publicly traded shares are not being researched or recommended at all by brokerage houses. Reports or market letters are now rarely prepared or distributed on them (except by the investment advisory services), and smaller, early phase companies with low-priced inactive issues get no notice at all. This situation is further aggravated by the departure of hundreds of small broker/dealer firms that entered the business in the 1960s, primarily to underwrite new issues. When the fad was over, they disappeared from view. As a result, hundreds of smaller secondary companies that went public in that era have no market sponsorship today. Stocks are like any other consumer goods; you have to know about them before you will buy them. Today, nobody is telling the story of these second- or third-tier publicly owned corporations.

Not only are earlier underwritings of fledgling enterprises languishing and neglected in the over-the-counter market, but there is almost no activity in the origination and distribution of new issues. In 1969, more than 1000 new issues were publicly offered; in 1977, fewer than thirty of any substance (not counting Regulation As and small local mining and corporate promotions).

These stocks, however, are far and away the best bet for the small speculator—someone who has perhaps only $500 to $1000 to invest.

In addition to the general absence of dissemination of information about thousands of lesser-known or regional companies, there is an adverse attitude toward doing business in the lower-priced shares of second- or third-tier corporations, whose shares trade inactively. Roadblocks are set up by major brokerage firms, and thus they may:

1. Decline to accept or execute an unsolicited buy order on a stock selling below $5.
2. Request a statement by the customer that he or she is buying the stock "on his own" and not on the basis of any recommendation, expressed or implied, by the firm.
3. Ban the solicitation by customers' brokers of orders in "below $5" issues or deny commission credit on any such orders, if taken and executed.
4. Execute orders in low-priced OTC stocks only "at the market" and not at a specified price.
5. Maintain a policy that "our brokers will attempt to dissuade clients from buying low-priced or unseasoned stocks"; and to warn clients about the speculative perils inherent in such issues.
6. Require a written memo from customers' brokers citing the basis for recommending all low-priced issues, especially those trading in the OTC market.
7. Deny margin accommodation on stocks selling below $5.
8. Make unavailable, or provide reluctantly, statistical data on these mini-stocks.

All or many of these steps have been taken by firms not as a deliberate disservice to clients but because their research departments are simply not equipped to provide accurate current information about issues not regularly followed; because low-priced issues are a nuisance, since they require just as much paperwork as higher-priced, more profitable issues, and requests for quotes on mini-stocks tie up traders' phones during busy markets; and because firms prefer, where possible, to limit their recommendations and executions to seasoned securities with broad trading markets and extensive research data available, rather than in low prices and highly volatile securities.

Such firms are also concerned that their newer brokers may not be properly equipped by knowledge or training to counsel clients in the purchase or sale of risky lower-priced issues with thin markets; and in following the policy "know your investor," they may decide that penny stocks have no place in conservative portfolios. Finally, they may be concerned about possible lawsuit if a customer buys a low-priced stock that "goes sour" and then blames the firm for "putting him into it."

Stock exchanges, too, have exercised surveillance over low-priced shares, especially if there appeared evidence of manipulation. To dampen speculative ardor, the AMEX, in 1968, asked four companies either to reverse split their shares (bringing them into a higher-priced trading range) or face delisting. They were delisted!

We have stressed the current plight of the low-priced or basement-level stocks because we think Wall Street errs in discouraging trading in this sector. Most new young companies start out with low-priced shares. Making venture capital available to finance or expand smaller enterprises is an essential function of capitalism. Denying market access to these mini-stocks may prevent thousands of investors, well aware of the risks involved, from making killings or even fortunes on shares that start out at low prices.

Look at the results of early investment in some originally low-priced items. You could have bought 100 shares of Occidental Petroleum at $.20 a share in 1956. That $20 investment grew to over $13,000 by June 1968. A hundred shares of Monogram Industries bought at 1½ in 1965 grew to $5700 in market value in 1968. Between 1962 and 1968, a 100-share lot of Ogden Corp. grew from $425 to over $5200. Control Data sold at $2 in 1958 and as high as $156 in 1968. In the 1920s, Tabulating and Recording Co., a predecessor of IBM, sold at $4 a share! There are hundreds of other examples of stock like these, bought for peanuts by individuals willing to take a chance, that made killings or built fortunes.

It really didn't take a genius in the 1950s to imagine that Xerox, with its labor-saving automatic copying machine, would be a big success. Early perception of the virtues of adhesive and masking tapes might have made a fortune for you in 3M stock. Tropicana, transporting juice rather than whole oranges to your breakfast table, obviously had a winning idea. H & R Block found a major need and filled it.

Look around today for a young company with a new product or service—a mini-computer, a patented medical or surgical instrument, a new process converting wastes into fuel, a profitable new gold-mining process like ERGO, a new proprietary medicine, or a style or fabric that could replace denim. The opportunities are always there! Plan to lodge a small percentage of your investment funds in bold venturesome stocks. Spread your dollars over four or five and you're likely to get at least one good performer among them.

In looking about for gainful mini-stocks, here is some of the information you should get:

1. Where the company is located and how long it has been in business.
2. Something about the kind of business it's in and its products, services, patents, processes; its customers and markets.
3. Latest twelve months' earning statement and balance sheet.
4. Names of principal officers and some opinion as to their management capability.
5. Market range of stock in the past two years, and some indications of trading volume.
6. Current economic factors that might favor (or disfavor) company operations.
7. Does management own a substantial amount of stock (20 percent or more)?
8. Any special feature of the company: a patent, tax-loss carry forward, valuable realty, forest or mineral resources, etc.
9. Reasonable estimate of net profits in the next twelve months.

Of course this list is not a complete one, but it provides guidelines for data to help you reach an investment decision.

In current security markets there are probably over 40,000 stock issues traded, or at least quoted, each week. Of these, about 7500 are active—quoted daily on the various exchanges and in the OTC market. Of the entire 40,000, probably 10,000 sell at $5 or below (1/30/78), so that you have plenty to choose from.

In this market sector you can find not only shares of small, young, and growing companies possibly en route to impressive stature and profitability, but old and tired companies whose fortunes have waned. Pennsylvania Railroad paid dividends for over a hundred years and sold above 80 in 1968. It is now Penn Central, in bankruptcy, and the stock trades around 1½. Hy-Gain Electronics Corporation common traded at $1 in 1974. It was one of the leaders in the booming citizens band radio industry which came on strong in 1975–76. Company earnings shot up and a million shares of Hy-Gain common were underwritten at 19¼ in February 1976. The company is now in Chapter 11 and the stock quotes at ¼! Brunswick, a leader in the roaring bowling industry in the 1960s, reached 74⅞ in 1961. It dove to 6 in 1966 when the fad faded.

A classic group of stocks that went "down on their luck" were the real estate investment trusts. In the early seventies, about 170 of these REITs went public with issues of bonds and shares of beneficial interest. The idea was attractive: to gather important and substantial realty equity holdings or mortgages under one roof in trust form, so that when 90 percent, or more, of available income was paid each year to trust shareholders, the trust itself escaped federal income tax liability. The income "passed through" to investors without double taxation. It sounded wonderful, and REIT securities (debentures and stocks) were offered by some of the nation's best investment banking houses. The shares enjoyed short-run popularity. Chase Manhattan Mortgage and Trust sold as high as 57. You can buy it on NYSE at ¾ November 3, 1978. Continental Mortgage Investors had 20,838,000 shares of beneficial interest outstanding. They once sold at 23. Today the company is in Chapter 11 and the shares fetch $.75!

The REIT industry involves over $20 billion in properties and mortgages. Some of the more conservative REITs made out well and continued to pay rewarding dividends. Even those now in trouble or in bankruptcy may again prove gainful, as the values of condominiums and other properties rise in an inflationary economy, and as creditors work out reorganizations of debt, and accept lower interest returns.

Indeed, for the bold, bankruptcies in many fields are worth exploring. In the reorganizations that follow, some dismally low-priced shares can rack up exciting percentage gains. Wall Street seems to have a unique capability to "overreact" both to bad and good news!

The message of this chapter is simple. You should not neglect consideration of a security for speculative purposes merely because a big brokerage firm does not recommend it or even disfavors it. Opportunities in low-priced shares are found in almost every industry or market sector. You can purchase such stocks from discount houses.

Your low-priced stock shopping list can include new issues, warrants, mining shares, spinoffs, shares issued in reorganization and companies on their way up, as well as those steeped in misery, misfortune, or mismanagement. If you have courage, patience, and common sense, and get the information you need to make a logical market decision, then you may add zest to your life and enhance your net worth. But one last word: you must diversify. A low-priced stock may do one of two things: go up or blow up!

# A List of Lazarus Securities

"Stocks to Come Up from the Dead"—Buy and hold for the 1980s

| Company | Stock Exchange | Ticker Symbol | Price (Nov. 3, 1978) |
|---|---|---|---|
| Action Industries, Inc. | ASE | ACX | 3 |
| Acton Corporation | ASE | ATN | 8⅝ |
| Adams Drug Company | NYSE | ADG | 4 |
| Alberto-Culver Co. | NYSE | ACV | 6¾ |
| American Airlines, Inc. Warrants | NYSE | AMR | 5⅜ |
| Ampex Corporation | NYSE | APX | 13 |
| Brauch-Foster Corp. | ASE | BFO | 2⅝ |
| Bayuk Cigars, Inc. | NYSE | BYK | 9½ |
| Bell Industries | NYSE | BI | 5⅜ |
| Beverly Enterprises | ASE | BEV | 6¼ |
| Bluebird, Inc. | NYSE | BBX | 5½ |
| Brooks & Perkins, Inc. | ASE | BPI | 12¾ |
| Buell Industries, Inc. | ASE | BUE | 12⅛ |
| Butler International | NYSE | BTL | 19⅛ |
| Christiana Companies | ASE | CST | 6 |
| Clark Cons, Industries | ASE | CLK | 4¼ |
| Coca-Cola Bottling, N.Y. | NYSE | KNY | 6⅝ |
| Compo Industries, Inc. | ASE | CEM | 9 |
| Compudyne Corporation | ASE | CDC | 1½ |
| Continental Materials | ASE | CUO | 5⅜ |
| Crest-Foam Corporation | ASE | CFO | 2⅝ |
| DCL, Inc. | ASE | DCL | 3⅜ |
| Dictaphone Corporation | NYSE | DC | 14⅝ |
| Dynamics Corp. of America | NYSE | DYA | 5⅜ |
| Elgin National Industries | NYSE | ENW | 20⅞ |
| Federal Signal Corp. | NYSE | FSS | 12¾ |
| Gable Industries, Inc. | NYSE | GBI | 4⅞ |
| General Steel Industries | NYSE | GSI | 7⅞ |
| Gleason Works | NYSE | GLE | 17⅜ |
| Golden West Homes | ASE | GWH | 8¼ |
| Great American Industries | ASE | GRI | 7 |
| Greenman Bros., Inc. | ASE | GMN | 2⅛ |
| Hartz Mountain Corp. | ASE | HTZ | 12¼ |

| Company | Stock Exchange | Ticker Symbol | Price (Nov. 3, 1978) |
|---|---|---|---|
| Harvey Group, Inc. | ASE | HRA | 2¾ |
| Heinicke Instruments Co. | ASE | HEI | 4 |
| Heck's Inc. | NYSE | HEX | 9¼ |
| Helene Curtis Industries | NYSE | HC | 8½ |
| Holly Corporation | ASE | HOC | 6¼ |
| Hycel, Inc. | ASE | HCL | 3⅜ |
| International Banknote | ASE | IBK | 3¼ |
| Jupiter Industries | ASE | JUP | 7⅞ |
| Kaufman & Broad, Inc. | NYSE | KB | 6⅜ |
| Kellogg Company | NYSE | K | 19⅞ |
| Kin-Ark Corporation | ASE | KIN | 3 |
| Landmark Land Co. | ASE | LML | 5⅝ |
| Lawter Chemicals, Inc. | NYSE | LAQ | 9½ |
| Lehigh Valley Industries | NYSE | LEH | 2⅛ |
| Logicon, Inc. | ASE | LGN | 11½ |
| LTV Corporation (THE) | NYSE | LTV | 7 |
| Mattel, Inc. | NYSE | MAT | 7⅜ |
| MEI Corporation | NYSE | MEI | 9⅛ |
| National Education Corp. | ASE | NSY | 6¾ |
| National Homes Corp. | NYSE | NHX | 2⅜ |
| NVF Company | NYSE | NVF | 6⅛ |
| Pan-American World Airways, Inc. | NYSE | PN | 7½ |
| Rapid-American Corporation | NYSE | RPD | 12¾ |
| Recognition Equipment | OC | RECE | 8⅜ |
| Shaer Shoe Corp. | ASE | SHS | 5⅛ |
| Speed-O-Print Bus. Machines | ASE | SBM | 4 |
| Technical Tape, Inc. | ASE | TTI | 2½ |
| Technitrol, Inc. | ASE | TNL | 4 |
| Trans World Airlines, Inc. | NYSE | TWO | 18¾ |
| U.S. Home Corp. | NYSE | UH | 7⅞ |

WE ADVISE ALL READERS: IT SHOULD NOT BE
ASSUMED THAT SPECULATIONS LISTED ABOVE
WILL BE UNIFORMLY PROFITABLE!

# 13

## The Billion-Share
## Short Squeeze

Among the elements in the market renaissance we envision is the increased acceptance of all types of leverage. Leverage is best described as the use of other people's money to generate larger earnings or gains for your money. Perhaps the most common example of leverage is the real estate mortgage. You may buy a $100,000 house, putting up $50,000 of your own money and borrowing $50,000 on a mortgage. Each dollar of yours then does the work of two dollars. Should you sell the house for $120,000, the $20,000 gain would represent a 40 percent return on your $50,000, but it would represent only a 20 percent return, had you put up the entire $100,000 to buy the house yourself originally.

When you buy stock on margin you enjoy a leverage,

presently that of 2 to 1 with a 50 percent margin requirement, whereby you supply 50 percent of the cost of your
investment and the broker lends you the other 50 percent
at interest. (In 1929, with only a 10 percent requirement,
the leverage ratio was 10 to 1!)

Also, the capitalization of companies creates leverage for
stockholders. If a company, for example, has $3 million in
debt (other people's money) and $1 million in outstanding
common stock, the leverage for shareholders is 3 to 1.

Another leverage device is the warrant (issued by a corporation). This is a negotiable certificate permitting its owner
to buy a share or shares (or fractions of shares) of common
stock in a company at a specific price and during a limited
period of time. The now existing warrant to buy one share
of Greyhound Corp. at $23.50 through 1/15/80 is a good
example. On November 16, 1978, the stock sold at 11½ and
the warrant at $.50. The virtue of warrants is that they per-
mit you to share in the market rise (or decline) of a given
stock with a low capital outlay. Warrants, however, pay no
dividends and you must be a very attentive trader, watching
the market like a hawk, in order to succeed in trading
warrants.

The best time to buy warrants is in the early stages of a
bull market, preferably at a warrant price of one-third (or
less) of the prevailing price of the related common stock.
There are more than 450 warrants available for your purchase in the market—a few are listed on NYSE, more on
the Amex; and most are trading over the counter. Warrants
are a splendid vehicle for maximizing your profits in bull
markets.

## Options

The most popular high-leverage market vehicle today is the *call option*, introduced in 1973. It was first traded on the Chicago Board Options Exchange (CBOE). It is the first cousin of the warrant.

The call option differs from other security types in that it (1) is not issued as a certificate or bond of any corporation; (2) has no participation in the sale, liquidation, or distribution of any corporate assets; (3) never pays a dividend or interest; (4) has no voting rights; (5) is not limited to any specific number of units outstanding; (6) expires within a short period—generally nine months; (7) limits possible loss to the price paid for the option. These options are now available on about 220 different stocks and are traded on the Chicago Board of Trade and on the American, Philadelphia, Midwest, and Pacific Stock Exchanges.

The call option gives its owner the right to buy 100 shares of a particular stock, actively traded on an exchange, at a specific price and for a limited period of time. The purchase price (called the *striking price*) may be the current quotation, or several points higher. The stock is called the *underlying security*; the party originating the option is the *option writer*; the party who pays the money is the *option buyer*; and the price he pays is called the *premium*.

The call is usually originated by the outright owner of a given stock. Suppose Mr. Rich owns 100 shares of General Electric paying $2.60 a share in dividend. Mr. Rich would like to increase his income so he sells, on January 2, 1978, a nine-months call option at $50 on his 100 shares to gain $500 (less a $25 commission). The option buyer is willing to pay $500 because he believes that General Electric will advance 30 points within 9 months to $80. If it does, the profit on the $500 option will be $2500 (on 100 shares from $50 to $60). Thus by investing only $500, the option buyer stands to make almost the same profit as does the outright holder of 100 shares, but with only a tenth of the capital at risk.

The merit of a call option is that it enables the owner to participate in the price increase of the named stock with far less money invested than if he bought the stock outright. In the case of Bally, a $500 call can make the same capital gain realized by the owner of 100 shares of stock, but using a $500 investment instead of $4100. However, if the stock goes down below the option price and remains there, the entire $500 would be lost. In other words, the subject stock must go up for you to win.

In bear markets, most call options will lose money, and therefore the risks must be carefully weighed. The option speculation approach we recommend is that of the East-West Pool technique, in which you speculate only with the interest earned from the principal of your conservative capital base pool. The limitation of time is the principle hazard in option speculation. The option buyer can, however, sell his holding for whatever it would bring any time during the allotted period.

Some options (like warrants) have been amazingly profitable. Bally options on the stock at 40 could have been bought in early 1978 at $4 and as high as $30 apiece in a matter of weeks. They plummeted disastrously, however, when Bally descended from a 71 high, down to 31 in November 1978.

Most options are sold by stockholders. Some daring souls,

however, sell what are called "naked" options—that is, they don't own the stock but merely are willing to bet it will not go up! If a person sells a naked option his broker will insist that he lodge sufficient money or securities with the firm to assure fulfillment of the option contract. Imagine these naked option writers in a runaway bull market—they must buy the stock quickly, possibly at a substantial loss, to cover their position. Sometimes option stocks will leap higher in a single day than the entire premium a naked option writer receives, causing instant panic. Therefore, naked option writing is one of the riskiest market operations for an investor.

Options can provide a swift leveraged "ride." They work best in bull markets when popular stocks are rising dramatically. In the past, such "swingers" as Polaroid, Bally Manufacturing, and Houston Oil and Minerals have rewarded option owners well in confident markets. Speculation in this area has become a significant source of income to brokerage firms and has notably expanded trading volume in popular issues. More important, options in the coming boom represent a powerful catalyst to explosive upside price movements.

The exponential growth in the options market has now created a sleeping giant, since a major portion of the shares represented by options are naked (uncovered), the option market has created the greatest "short position" in stock market history! As hundreds of options series, particulraly naked options, are written and traded, thousands of individuals may be driven into the share market to cover their positions.

The forces that motivate modern economic man are spotlighted in the option market. Here, overnight riches (and overnight financial disasters) await avid speculators.

## The Short Squeeze

Option volume is soaring into new all-time highs. In fact, the options traffic has grown 5000 percent since its inception six years ago, and on many days the volume of shares represented by options trading exceeds the volume on the N.Y. Stock Exchange. If option volume continues to grow at such a pace, there will be a greater tendency for the stock market to move up with vigor, due to option short squeezes.

A small ripple in the stock market is like a tidal wave to many uncovered option writers who are trying to capitalize on short-term price movements. In an uptrending market the decisions made by these option speculators will surely stimulate major covering or hedging in the equity market.

Naked option writers (now estimated by the Chicago Board of Trade to be an average of 23 percent of all option writers) will scramble to buy stock. As one set of naked option writers covers, there will be a newer group of naked option writers who think the market is too high. With every wave of new highs, the new option shorts will scramble to cover. We will find that these short squeezes will occur sporadically, marked by sudden price moves along with record high volume on the New York Exchange. In fact, this volume expansion has become characteristic in the past few years.

As shown on Chart 9, the price explosion in Resorts International and Bally Mfg. illustrates what can happen as stock prices reach all-time highs. Once an all-time high is hit, the short positions—or, in the case of Bally Mfg., the naked option writers—rush to cover and buy the shares they do not have. Since all of these positions are put to the test within a few days, it is no wonder prices explode.

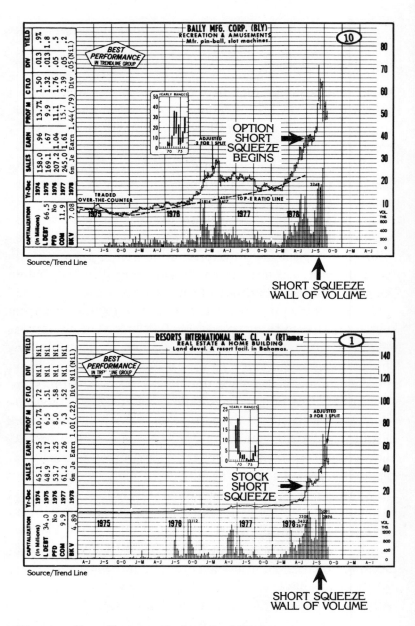

(Courtesy Trendline, 345 Hudson St., N.Y. 10014)

Repeatedly the naked option writers will be put to the squeeze, and the covered writers forced into holding long positions. As prices move up and options across the board go "in the money," all positions will have to be covered or at least hedged. (Every call option written is, in effect, a short sale.)

We are moving into a period when short squeeze action may not be limited to a particular stock or group of stocks, but emerge as an across-the-board phenomenon. As prices reach all-time highs, each short position becomes a loser, while every long position ever taken becomes a winner. This creates a squeeze on the shorts all at once. The result will be a dynamic surge in prices because more than a billion shares have been eliminated from the market's floating supply, due to the option market. The trigger point may appear when the Dow exceeds its past high of 1070. The developing panic to cover could cause a rash of equity buying, sending the prices of stocks spiraling upwards.

Sensational volume will then create front page news!

After years of sideways motion, and of dull, inactive markets—after years of eroding stock prices—America will explode in the 1980s from its longest reconsolidation in modern history (as identified by the Dow). This will create a confident attitude, ushering in a new boom on Wall Street and the emergence of a new generation of investors. All of a sudden the iceberg of pessimism will melt as the Dow sizzles to new all-time highs.

In the 1980s millions of investors will strive to be Dow-beaters, to outperform the averages, to outsmart the crowd. If history repeats itself the Dow will chart a pathway to unrivaled prosperity for the shrewd, the thrifty, the informed, and the patient. The future is in your hands. . . .

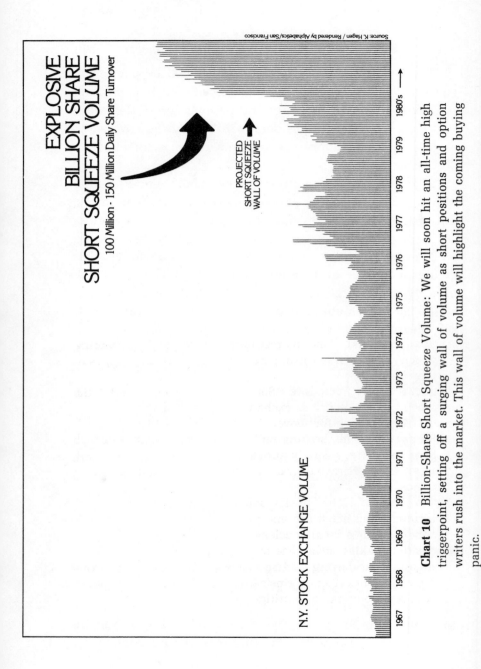

**Chart 10** Billion-Share Short Squeeze Volume: We will soon hit an all-time high triggerpoint, setting off a surging wall of volume as short positions and option writers rush into the market. This wall of volume will highlight the coming buying panic.

# Glossary

ACCRUED INTEREST   The interest on a bond, note, or debenture which has been earned since the last interest payment thereon.

AMERICAN STOCK EXCHANGE   Sometimes called "the Curb," the second major securities exchange in New York.

AMEX   Abbreviation for above.

AMORTIZATION   The "writing off" of an asset over a period of time, usually at a certain annual percentage.

ANALYST   A professional evaluator of securities and economic trends.

ANNUAL REPORT   The official statement of assets, liabilities, earnings, and net worth and progress (if any), of a corporation, covering a fiscal or calendar year.

ARBITRAGE   Taking advantage of existing price differentials by simultaneous buying and selling (usually in different markets) of identical or intrinsically equivalent assets (currencies, commodities, or securities).

ASSETS   Anything a corporation owns or is owed.

AVERAGES   The various barometers of stock price trends. Best known are the Dow Jones Industrial Average, made up of thirty major stocks; *New York Times* Average of fifty stocks; Standards and Poor's Average of four hundred twenty-five industrial stocks; NYSE Common Stock Index, a composite of all "listed" common stocks.

BALANCE SHEET   A financial statement revealing the assets, liabilities, capital, and net worth of a company on a specific date.

BANKRUPTCY   Where a corporation's liabilities exceed its assets and it is unable to meet its current obligations. There are two kinds: Chapter 11, Voluntary—where an accommodation with creditors may be worked out, and Chapter 10, Involuntary—where assets under court order are placed in the hands of a referee for disposition to satisfy creditors (usually but not always).

BEAR   A person who thinks stocks are going down, and who may sell stock "short" to back up his opinions.

BEAR MARKET   A declining one.

BID-AND-ASKED   A quotation of the best price which will be paid, and the lowest-priced offering of a security at a given moment.

BIG BOARD   The New York Stock Exchange.

BLUE CHIP   The common stock of a major company, with a long record of earnings and dividends.

BLUE SKY LAWS   Laws in many states protecting investors against being sold a slice of "the blue sky," i.e., a fraudulent, mythical, or misrepresented security.

BOARD ROOM   Sitting room for stock traders in a broker's office.

BOILER ROOM   A place where second-rate or worthless securities are sold to the gullible—usually over the phone.

BOND   The long-term obligation of a corporation to repay a given sum (usually in $1,000 denominations) on a given date, with a specified rate of interest to be paid at regular intervals until then. Bonds can be debentures (unsecured), or protected by collateral, lien, or mortgage on corporate property.

BOND PRICES    Quotations, given as percentages of par value.

BOOK VALUE    All the assets of a company, less all liabilities and the par value of preferred stocks (if any) divided by the number of common shares outstanding.

BROKER    A financial agent associated with a member of a stock exchange or a broker/dealer firm, who executes orders in securities or commodities on a commission basis.

BULL    A person believing that the market will rise, and aiming to profit if it does.

CALL OPTION    A contract to buy 100 shares of a stock at a specified price, for a limited period of time.

CALLABLE    A bond or preferred stock that may be redeemed and retired under certain conditions and at a specified price.

CAPITAL ASSETS    The fixed assets of a company, a factory, office building, plant, warehouse, trucks, etc.

CAPITAL GAIN OR LOSS    Profit or loss realized when a security (or other asset) is sold.

CAPITAL STOCK    The shares which represent the ownership of, or equity in, a company.

CAPITALIZATION    The entire amount of all securities (debt and equity) issued by a corporation.

CASH FLOW    The net income of a company (for a given period) to which are added depletion, depreciation, amortization charges, and nonrecurring charges to reserves; frequently stated "per share."

CATS AND DOGS    Low-priced stocks of dubious worth.

CBOE    Chicago Board Option Exchange.

CERTIFICATES OF DEPOSIT (CDs)    Short interest-bearing obligations of banking institutions, secured by deposits.

CHARTS    Statistical data about prices, volume, and trends in different stocks, portrayed graphically, hopefully to indicate the future direction of prices.

COLLATERAL    Property, most frequently securities, pledged to secure interest and repayment of a loan.

COMMERCIAL PAPER    The short-term notes or obligations of substantial corporations, maturing customarily within 12 months' time.

COMMISSION    The fee charged by a broker to execute an order to buy or sell.

COMMON STOCKS    The ownership or equity interest in a corporation, with a claim on assets or earnings, coming after preferred stocks, notes, bonds, or other indebtedness.

CONGLOMERATE    A company which has accumulated as subsidiaries a group of companies in many different and unrelated lines of business.

CONTROL    The group owning enough stock (customarily 51 percent or more), or influencing enough stockholders, to direct the affairs of a corporation.

CONVERTIBLE    A bond or preferred stock, which may, under certain conditions, be exchanged for common stock, usually in the same company.

CORPORATION    A legally organized intangible organization operating (usually) under a state charter with (1) unlimited life, (2) limited liability, and (3) transferable certificates representing shares of ownership.

COUPON BOND    One which pays interest semi-annually by means of detachable coupons which can be cashed when due.

CUMULATIVE PREFERRED    A stock which may pay at a later date any omitted regular dividends, and on which all past due dividends must be paid before the common stock can receive any distribution.

CURRENT ASSETS    Assets in cash, receivables, short-term securities, and items collectible and convertible into cash within a year.

CURRENT LIABILITIES    What a company owes that must be paid within a year.

CUSTOMER'S MAN    A representative of a stock exchange firm.

CUT A MELON    To declare a substantial extra dividend, usually in stock.

CYCLICAL STOCKS   Those whose earnings tend to fluctuate with the business cycle.

DEBENTURE   A kind of bond, unsecured by lien or mortgage on any specific property.

DELISTED   When a security is removed from trading on a stock exchange, and reverts to the OTC market.

DEPLETION   A bookkeeping charge against earnings to mark the lower remaining value of a natural resource holding (coal, oil, minerals, timber) after some part of it has been removed, extracted, or exhausted.

DEPRECIATION   A bookkeeping charge against earnings to write down the cost of an asset over its useful life.

DIRECTOR   A person elected by company shareholders to be a member of its Board of Directors and a maker of corporate policies and decisions.

DIVERSIFICATION   The spreading of investments among many different securities and industries.

DIVIDEND   A payment authorized by a Board of Directors, either in cash or in stock, pro rata among shareholders. Usually a distribution made from current or past profits.

DOLLAR COST AVERAGING   Applying a level sum of money each year, say $1000, to the purchase of as many shares of a stock as those dollars will buy at then-prevailing prices.

DOW THEORY   An attempt to project market trends on the basis of the correlated past market action of 30 industrial and 20 transportation stocks.

ECONOMIST   A social scientist, often in error but seldom in doubt.

EQUITY   The interest in a company represented by ownership of either (or both) its common or preferred stock.

EX DIVIDEND (X)   Indicates that the stock, if bought, does not carry with it the dividend most recently declared.

EXTRA   Any declaration in stock or cash above regular or customary dividend distribution.

FEDERAL RESERVE BOARD   The quasi-government agency controlling the supply and price of money and regulating installment credit and margin loans.

FISCAL YEAR   The official accounting year of a corporation (usually), when it does not coincide with the calendar year.

FIXED CHARGES   Fixed expenses of a corporation which must be paid whether earned or not—most commonly interest charges or rentals.

FLOOR   The trading area on a stock exchange.

FUNDAMENTAL ANALYSIS   Evaluation of a stock on the basis of its earnings, assets, profit margins, dividends, and investment stature.

FUNDED DEBT   Long-term interest-bearing obligations of a company, most commonly bonds and debentures.

GILT-EDGED   A high-grade bond, so called because it referred originally to issues payable (before 1933) in dollars convertible into gold.

GOING PUBLIC   The public offering of a company's securities for the first time.

GROWTH STOCK   A company whose sales, earnings, and net worth are expanding at an unusual rate.

GTC   An order good until cancelled (or executed).

INSIDER   A person or corporation owning 10 percent or more of the stock of a public company, who must report to SEC each month any substantial changes in holdings.

INTEREST   The price paid for use or rental of money, expressed as a percentage per annum.

INVESTMENT BANKER   An individual or a firm buying securities for resale to others. Also called an underwriter.

INVESTMENT COUNSEL   An individual or firm paid a fee to advise and/or manage investment accounts.

INVESTMENT TRUST   A company which gathers funds from individuals, and which invests these funds in a portfolio of diversified securities, professionally managed. There are "open end" trusts (called mutual funds) whose outstanding shares vary in number from day to day.

LAMB   A gullible investor.

LEVERAGE   Using other people's money to generate earnings or gain for you, as when large amounts of senior securities exist in a corporate capitalization, ahead of its common stock. Leverage is also created by using borrowed money to buy stocks (or a house with a mortgage).

LIABILITIES   Any and all legal claims against a company.

LIEN   A mortgage or other legal claim against property to secure a debt.

LIQUIDITY   The capability of an investment to be converted quickly into cash. Checking and savings account deposits are highly liquid; so are CDs, and commercial paper and prime short-term securities (municipal, government, or corporate notes).

LISTED STOCK   Shares trading on any stock exchange (most commonly the New York, American, and regional stock exchanges).

LONG   Means that you own a specific security or securities, as opposed to a short position where you sell what you don't own.

MANAGEMENT   The officers of a company and the board of directors which elects them.

MANIPULATION   The illegal "rigging" of stock prices by artificial stimulation, sometimes involving the spread of incorrect information.

MARGIN   The sum of money or value of securities deposited with a broker to purchase securities. Margin requirements (currently 50 percent of the cost of securities purchased) are determined at intervals by the Federal Reserve Board. Margin purchase is designed to enable a person to buy more securities than his own resources would permit.

MARGIN CALL   A broker's request to put up more money or collateral to protect security holdings that have declined, and that were purchased in part on borrowed money.

MARKET ORDER   An order to buy or sell at the best obtainable price then prevailing.

MERGER   When two or more companies are joined together.

MUNICIPALS   A generic germ for bonds issued by counties, cities, states, districts, or public authorities, usually with the interest payments exempt from federal taxation.

MUTUAL FUND   *See:* Investment Trust.

NEW ISSUE   The first public offering of a bond or stock.

NEW YORK STOCK EXCHANGE   The world's leading auction market for securities.

NYSE   Abbreviation for above.

ODD LOT   A small amount of stock, customarily less than 100 shares.

OPEN END FUND   A mutual fund or investment trust wherein shares are bought or sold only by the trust, with the amount of publicly held shares constantly changing as new shares are bought and old shares redeemed.

OVER-THE-COUNTER   The largest, and a nationwide, telephone and electronic market for those securities not regularly traded on any exchange.

OTC   Abbreviation for above.

PAPER PROFIT   Unrealized indicated gain on a security still held.

PAR VALUE   Face or nominal value of a security.

PENNY SHARES   Customarily those selling at $1.00 or less.

PERFORMANCE STOCK   One that gains spectacularly in price (or is expected to!).

PER SHARE NET   Total net earnings of a company after taxes, for a given period, divided by the number of common shares outstanding.

POINT   A point is $1.00 on stocks or $10 on a bond.

PORTFOLIO   The total security holdings of an individual or institution.

PREFERRED STOCK   A stock having a claim on a company's earnings or assets, ahead of its common stock, and usually entitled to dividends at a fixed rate.

PREMIUM   The amount by which a bond or preferred stock

sells above its face amount, or a new issue sells above its offering price.

PRICE/EARNINGS RATIO   The current price of a stock, divided by the per-share net earnings of the issuing company, for the most recently reported twelve-month period. (Also called "P/E Multiple.")

PRIME RATE   The interest rate charged by banks to their best customers on unsecured loans.

PRINCIPAL   A person or firm who buys and sells for his own account.

PROSPECTUS   A summary of all the pertinent history, facts, and figures about a company and the people who run it, prior to a new securities offering. By law, a prospectus must be presented to a possible buyer in advance of any purchase.

PROXY   Designation, by a stockholder, of someone else to represent him at a stockholder's meeting.

PUTS AND CALLS   Options to buy (a call) or to sell (a put) a certain number of shares of a stock at fixed prices for limited periods of time.

QUOTATION   The bid-and-asked price of a security.

RED HERRING   An early prospectus draft, omitting the offering price of the issue.

REGISTERED REPRESENTATIVE   A person approved by the Stock Exchange to handle orders for the purchase or sale of securities for clients. Also called an Account Executive and, formerly, a Customer's Man or Customer's Broker.

REFINANCING   The issuance of new securities to refund outstanding ones or to retire or extend a debt.

REGISTRATION   The filing of information about a forthcoming security offering with the Securities and Exchange Commission (national regulatory body) preliminary to preparation and printing of a prospectus.

RIGHTS   The privilege, given to a shareholder, to buy additional stock in a company for a limited time and at a special price.

SEC   The Securities and Exchange Commission, a federal organization for the regulation of the securities industry.

SECONDARY DISTRIBUTION    Offering of securities, previously issued, in which the company receives no share of the proceeds.

SENIOR SECURITIES    Bonds, notes, and preferred stocks ranking ahead of common stock.

SHORT SALE    Selling stock sold "short" (that is, not owned) with a view to buying it back later at a lower price; the stock is borrowed for delivery meanwhile (usually from a broker).

SHORT-TERM PAPER    Notes due within a year; commercial paper and certificates of deposit.

SINKING FUND    Money reserved by a corporation to buy in, and redeem, its own senior securities.

SPECIALIST    A floor member of an exchange designated to maintain an orderly market in specified securities and to act as a broker's broker.

SPECULATION    The employment of funds and assumption of risks primarily to create capital gains.

SPIN-OFFS    The delivery by a parent company to its stockholders of shares in another corporation.

SPLIT    Increasing the outstanding number of shares in a company by division of the existing ones.

STOCK DIVIDEND    A dividend paid not in cash but in securities.

STOP ORDER    An instruction to sell when and if a security reaches a certain price.

STREET NAME    Stock held in the name of a broker or nominee instead of the legal owner.

SWEETENER    A convertible privilege or a warrant attached to a senior security to make the issue more attractive and to thus reduce its interest or dividend rate.

SYNDICATE    A group of security firms cooperating with the underwriting firm in the distribution of a security issue.

TAX EXEMPT BOND    One with its interest payments exempt from federal income taxation.

TECHNICAL ANALYSIS    Evaluation of stocks on the basis of their recent market performance, volume, and price trends.

THIN MARKET   One in which there are few bids and offerings and (often) wide "spreads" between them.

TICKER   The electric device which immediately reports and transmits on tape prices and volumes of security transactions.

TIPS   Confidential urgings to buy certain securities, supposed to be based on information "from the horse's mouth."

TRADING POST   U-shaped booths on the floor of the NYSE, each one assigned to trade about 75 different stocks.

TRADING SYMBOLS   The abbreviations containing no more than three letters for listed stocks; sometimes four for OTC issues.

TRANSFER   The official recording of change in ownership of a security, performed by a transfer agent.

TREASURY BILLS   Short-term (usually no longer than six months) interest-bearing obligations of the U.S. government.

TREASURY STOCK   Stock formerly outstanding but repurchased by the company.

UNLISTED   (*See* Over-the-Counter) Name given to those securities not listed on any exchange but traded over-the-counter.

UTILITIES   A broad classification of corporate monopolies, including gas, electric, telephone, and water companies.

WARRANT   A certificate authorizing its owner to buy a share, shares (or fractions) of common stock of a company at a specific price and during a specified time period.

WHEN ISSUED   A security trading regularly, but not available for actual delivery until some future date.

WIRE HOUSE   A NYSE member firm connected with its branch offices or correspondents by direct telephone or teletype circuits.

YIELD   The return on investment in a given security at its current price, expressed as a percentage. To determine the yield on a stock, divide the present indicated annual dividend by the market price of a single share.

# Index